MW00511780

Eve of Destruction

The Wild Life of Wendy O. Williams

Robin Eisgrau

NEW HAVEN PUBLISHING LTD

Eve of Destruction

Published 2020
First Edition
NEW HAVEN PUBLISHING LTD
www.newhavenpublishingltd.com
newhavenpublishing@gmail.com

All Rights Reserved
The rights of Robin Eisgrau, as the author of this work, have been asserted
in accordance with the Copyrights, Designs and Patents Act 1988.
No part of this book may be re-printed or reproduced or utilized in any
form or by any electronic, mechanical or other means, now unknown or
hereafter invented, including photocopying, and recording, or in any
information storage or retrieval system, without the written permission of
the Author and Publisher.

Front Cover image © Kevin Hodapp/Frank White Photo Agency

Cover design © Pete Cunliffe
pcunliffe@blueyonder.co.uk

Copyright © 2020 Robin Eisgrau
All rights reserved
ISBN: 978-1-912587-43-8

For the memory of Marc Crawford

Eve of Destruction

Content

Eve of Destruction

The Queen of Shock Rock

July 26, 1978, New York City
Downtown Manhattan, 9:00 PM.

Where the Bowery meets Bleecker Street, taxis cruise by but no one's hailing them. Disappointed cabbies shake their heads and head north.

The homeless men congregating on the sidewalk have maybe 15 cents between them.

Filing into legendary rock club CBGB is a stream of people who don't want to be anywhere else. The Plasmatics are performing tonight on the CBGB stage. This is one of their first shows. The lead singer of the Plasmatics is Wendy Orlean Williams.

Plasma is the root word of this band's name – implying, according to the dictionary definition and speaking in terms of anatomy, the liquid part of blood or lymph as distinguished from the suspended elements. In physics, plasma is a highly ionized gas containing an approximately equal number of positive ions and electrons. The suffix '-ics' connotes that the band members have something to do with the basic structure of this gas and blood – the life-giving fluid present in everyone's body – and that it's essential to them.

As patrons enter the club, hirsute CBGB patriarch Hilly Kristal stands near the front desk, observing who's constituting that night's audience. Bridge and tunnel punk rock fans eagerly hand over cash to pay their admission charge, while Lower East Side musicians haggle about being on the guest list.

Some of the club-goers are squeezing out of their teens and into their twenties, others are fending off 30 as best they can with youthful accoutrements: torn blue jeans and t-shirts, leather jackets, spiky hair, Converse Chuck Taylor sneakers or Dr. Martens bought at St. Marks Place punk boutique Trash and Vaudeville on their feet.

In the phone booth, a bleached-blonde girl in a pink striped t-shirt yells a stream of curses at her soon-to-be ex-boyfriend through the receiver. Above her, Joey Ramone is leaning against the pool table. A Ramones fan walks up to him and offers to buy him a drink. Joey says "ok" but he really doesn't care about that.

The interior walls of CBGB are dank, cavern-like, coated by the smoky grime patina from thousands of cigarettes smoked in the club since its opening years earlier. Dilapidated posters for bands who have taken the stage there in the past are tacked up, curling at their edges.

Hanging from the middle of the ceiling is a weathered parade of neon beer signs; some are broken and ancient-looking, others flicker with a little life left: Miller, Ballantine, Budweiser.

Sitting at a table with a friend, fashion designer Anna Sui stirs her drink with a swizzle stick as she observes the display of rock 'n' roll fashion in the club; taking note of the girls in spaghetti-strapped tank tops and vinyl miniskirts with colored tights or leopard-print pants and spike heeled boots. She sees boys in leather jackets decorated with studs and band buttons over ripped t-shirts – storing all these images in her encyclopedic music-inspired clothing imagination.

No Wave femme fatale Anya Phillips sits on a bar stool and talks about her latest PR concept into the ear of James Chance, lead singer of The Contortions, for whom she's the manager. Chance responds to her with a "maybe" look as he reaches for his whiskey.

A 20 year-old punk rocker guy from New Jersey, trying his best to look like Johnny Ramone, exclaims "What the fuck...?" as he stumbles over *something* on his way to the bathroom. He looks down and sees a guy passed out, not knowing that person is Legs McNeil, the rock scribe who would go on to co-author *Please Kill Me* with Gillian McCain – the definitive chronicle of CBGB's history almost

20 years later on. Jersey guy shrugs and heads downstairs; he's peed in the ghastly CBGB bathroom before, nothing fazes him.

As the Plasmatics prepare to start their set, lead singer Wendy O. Williams is psyching herself up for their first song, "Want You (Baby)." Her back is to the audience and she lightly bounces on the balls of her feet like a boxer, snapping her fingers. Wendy's hair is red and styled like a girl from the early Sixties; fluffy with bangs and flipped edges on either side of her head – sweet with a touch of mischief. Tonight Wendy wears a tight white t-shirt with PLASMATICS emblazoned on the front in thick black letters.

Clear plastic jeans cover Wendy's legs over neutral-colored underwear. She is wearing black knee high boots. Her appearance has a bit of punk naiveté. She would later describe her look in the early days of the Plasmatics as "America's dream girl gone nightmare." Guitarist Richie Stotts stands well over six feet tall, clad in a white butcher's coat with ersatz sergeant's stripes on the sleeve. Bassist Chosei Funahara is bald with a stringy mustache and drummer Stu Deutsch, sporting aviator sunglasses, looks like a teenager out past curfew.

The Plasmatics rip into "Want You (Baby)." Wendy grabs the microphone stand, strangling it, tossing it to and fro as she growls the song's lyrics. As Richie, Chosei and Stu crank out a pummeling onslaught of music that expands the definition of punk like a bubble gum bubble dotted with sharp spikes being blown by a furious child, Wendy steps away and dances in a shimmy, snapping her fingers once more and attacking the microphone again. It's as if she's channeling every angry Sunset Strip go-go dancer who was forbidden to speak while working as she roars in a guttural snarl. When the song is over, the audience applauds and cheers heartily.

When the Plasmatics appeared at CBGB that July night, as the Seventies were edging towards a close and the Reagan-era Eighties approached, their performance hinted at what would become their signature style of mayhem.

Wendy O. Williams soon emerged as the most outrageous female rock performer of her time.

When the Plasmatics performed, Wendy would often appear onstage topless, with bits of black electrical tape covering her nipples. Her breasts would be smeared with shaving cream. Her blonde hair would often be styled in a Mohawk, sometimes with the middle section or sides dyed black, sometimes tinted with a spot of pink and in a random ponytail. "We loved it," says Jean Beauvoir, bassist for the Plasmatics who replaced Chosei Funahara, speaking of Wendy's provocative onstage comportment. "This band was a perfect place for us to act out all the rebellion that we had and be who we wanted to be," he said in a 2019 interview.

During a Plasmatics concert, Wendy would demolish television sets with a sledgehammer or an axe, fire guns at speakers, slice apart an electric guitar with a chainsaw or blow up a Cadillac Coupe de Ville.

Often referred to as the "Queen of Shock Rock," Wendy was the only female rock singer of her time to wreak havoc onstage in such a fierce manner.

The objects that Wendy destroyed during Plasmatics performances were viewed by the band as representing toxic consumer culture and a society obsessed with materialism. As Wendy once stated, "Basically, I hate conformity. I hate people telling me what to do. It makes me want to smash things. So-called normal behavior patterns make me so bored, I could throw up! I don't like fashion. I don't like art. I do like smashing up expensive things. That makes me cum."

When Wendy performed, she was on her own pleasure and subversion rampage.

Unlike the female singers who came before her, Wendy didn't appear onstage looking as conventionally pretty as possible, singing a sweet song as she tried to win the hearts of those assembled who were expecting to be entertained by her. Her stage presence was confrontationally sexual, not coquettish or mincingly trying to please male members of her audience. Wendy's toplessness was not her putting her body on display and playing into an established idea of acceptable sexiness, like a typical stripper or a performer like

Madonna does. Instead, Wendy reveled in the fact that she had nothing to hide or be self-conscious of as a woman performer.

Male audience members have been known to shout out "show us your tits!" to women rock musicians but by coming out on stage with her breasts exposed (save for shaving cream or whipped cream and electrical tape), Wendy pre-empted such a sexist request. It was as if she was saying, "These are my tits and I'm topless for *myself*, not for you – so *fuck off*."

A woman choosing to bear her breasts not for male titillation purposes but for her own reasons has a chain of cultural meaning. In the one-woman play *Ain't I A Woman* based on former slave and human rights activist Sojourner Truth's famous speech and staged at New York's Circle In The Square Theater in the early 2000s, the actress portraying Truth bares her breast at a key point. She does this to prove wrong the male detractors who speculate that she is not even a woman.

In November of 2019, six topless women from the feminist group Femen protested at a demonstration in Madrid commemorating the legacy of Spain's former dictator Francisco Franco. They chanted "for fascism no honor and no glory" and that phrase was written across their chests. Upon scoring the winning goal in a championship match in the 1990s, U.S. Women's Soccer player Brandi Chastain immediately took off her shirt in a gesture of triumph. She *was* wearing a sports bra but this act was in a similar vein.

Wendy would also sometimes simulate masturbation onstage with a microphone – an act she would blithely dismiss to *People* magazine reporter Carol Wallace as "just a gesture – like Italians talking with their hands." At one point she got a tattoo on her arm that read "I Love Sex and Rock 'n' Roll."

"I'm a blatant exhibitionist and I always wanted to be a rock 'n' roll singer," Wendy told Phil Sutcliffe in an interview for British music magazine *Sounds* in 1980. "Now that I got the opportunity I'm thrilled. I mean I've never had so much fun in my life. I've never had so many orgasms in my life."

Sutcliffe then asks Wendy if she has orgasms on stage, to which she replies: "The energy, the whole thing, it…really, really gets my blood pumping, my adrenaline flowing, it gives me that instant orgasmic rush. It's just like fucking, *super*-fucking. Well, my panties are always wet. I can't help it *(chuckle)*. "

Later on, in the early 1990s, traces of Wendy's sexually confrontational performing style was seen in Lynn Breedlove, singer for the punk band Tribe 8, who would masturbate onstage using a dildo in an explicit manner. Also in the early '90s, the drummer for San Francisco-based band Her Majesty The Baby, a young woman, would play drums topless. Miley Cyrus's twerking kewpie-doll/cartoon-lewd performance alongside Robin Thicke at the 2013 MTV Video Music Awards can *maybe* be viewed as taking a cue from Wendy's simulating masturbation onstage nearly 35 years prior. When Wendy sang it was as if she destroyed all preconceived notions of how a woman *should* sing and sound. Her vocals were guttural, growling; the sound of a ferocious woman. Wendy always resisted people telling her to sing in a more radio-palatable, "pleasant" voice. "She was like Xena, Warrior Princess," reflects Ida Langsam, who was Wendy's publicist at one point as well as being the New York columnist for British hard rock/heavy metal magazine *Kerrang!*, "where Xena's this commanding powerful presence. You could worship her but you wouldn't try to touch her. Wendy would have been a warrior. She was a real heroine."

Courtney Love's raspy, wailing vocals have punk lineage connected to Wendy's ferocious singing. The Los Angeles-based all-female band L7's sound has a punk genesis that seemingly echoes Wendy's vocal style and there's even traces of Wendy's growl in alt-country diva Lucinda Williams's purring snarl (she's no relation to Wendy). A clip of a Lady Gaga SXSW performance shows a young woman with her onstage drinking green fluid and then making herself throw up on Gaga's chest. A commentary on bulimia? Perhaps -- an act that's disturbing to see as an audience member yet thousands of women and girls make themselves vomit every day. The addressing of a toxic aspect of society present in this performance would possibly get a nod of approval from Wendy.

RuPaul, the most well-known, modern-day drag performer, fronted a punk band in Atlanta in the early Eighties called Wee Wee

Pole and he cited Wendy O.Williams as an influence, saying, according to the *Afropunk* website: "I was inspired by bands like The B-52's, Wendy O. Williams (of Plasmatics), and my all-time favorite, Blondie," RuPaul said on a season 8 episode of his hit TV show *RuPaul's Drag Race*.

In the documentary *Wendy O. Williams and the Plasmatics: 10 Years of Revolutionary Rock and Roll*, British music journalist Malcom Dome talks about how uncompromising Wendy was – how she refused to make safe career moves by pandering to the people who wanted her to "sing for radio" and how she unflinchingly risked her life in performance. Dome speaks of Wendy's "force of charisma." Unlike typical star power where the audience is led in and seduced by a performer, "Wendy's charisma JUMPED out at you," Dome says.

As Wendy smashed apart television sets, blew up cars and sawed guitars in half, she was dubbed "The Dominatrix of the Decibels" and "The Queen of Shock Rock" in the press. When she destroyed these sought-after things she was telling her audience to stop devoting all their time and energy to acquiring big-ticket objects and to think for themselves; to not be sucked in by the lure of capitalist society's Pyrrhic prizes. As Plasmatics manager/creator Rod Swenson explained to *Noisey*, the online music division of *VICE*, as he discussed the role of shock in the Plasmatics' ethos: "Part of the assault on conformity and what we saw as blind worshipping of consumerism was shocking to people indoctrinated into it. People found it shocking to see and people respond to shock in different ways. Shock can move people from one place to another in a very good way, but other people become consciously or unconsciously defensive, and denial is one form of it. In this case, they don't see it."

Swenson has said in his interview with *Killdren* Magazine that Wendy was fearless and that was one of the remarkable aspects of her character. "That had a flipside to it too," he explains in this interview. "Because while things that would utterly terrify the ordinary person were just the things that would give her comfort and security, it was things that would give the ordinary person comfort – social conformity, "fitting in" etc. – that made her uncomfortable or feel threatened."

Musically, the Plasmatics blazed their own trail like sonic flamethrowers, playing a furious maelstrom of chaos that sounded like rock music celebrating its own destruction, led by Wendy's modern-age Valkyrie vocals. In the *Ten Years of Revolutionary Rock and Roll* documentary, the narrator remarks that the Plasmatics brought together punk and metal at a time when those factions of rock music were feuding.

Richie Stotts has said the Plasmatics' music "...wasn't punk, wasn't metal – it was something *else*." Jean Beauvoir elaborates: "I think it had certain elements of metal, based on the influences that we as musicians had each brought to the band. It created something different in the sound, which made it a morph of these different elements. The speed of punk, groove at times, the power of metal and a voice like no other."

The Plasmatics hybrid of loud, fast and heavy rock 'n' roll made their music a precursor to speed metal; their influence can be heard in bands such as Pantera and Slayer. Also, the Plasmatics' signature brand of stagecraft inspired bands that established themselves long after the Plasmatics broke up. Writing in *The Hartford Courant*, Roger Catlin cites Metallica's staged, spark-filled collapsing of a light tower on a late '90s tour as being inspired by the Plasmatics' own brand of spectacle.

In a March 2020 issue of *Revolver,* female metal-rap performer Dana Dentata lists Wendy as a substantial influence, calling her "The heavy-metal priestess" and going on to say, "seeing Wendy chainsaw a guitar at a young age inspired me to bring more to my performances. She defied the expectations of what a frontwoman should say/do and how they should look. She could be onstage with her tits out and carry so much masculinity with it. Nothing about her is male gaze. She created a world around her and had the coolest most interesting characters in her band with the sickest album covers. I love every single Plasmatics album. She will always feel like a spirit mother to me."

As the Plasmatics' notoriety grew in the late-1970s/early'80s New York music scene, they played larger venues such as The Ritz. Located on East 11 Street in New York's East Village since the late 1800s, when it was originally called Webster Hall (the name it would be known as again in the 1990s), The Ritz staged concerts by notable punk and new wave bands in the late 1970s and through the 1980s.

Seeing a concert at The Ritz was a hybrid experience of yesterday and now, as cutting-edge bands of the moment performed on a stage that was built a hundred some-odd years prior. When a concertgoer entered the venue they breathed in a mélange of stale cigarette smoke, old air conditioning and beer-soaked wood as they excitedly anticipated the evening's performance.

Famed rock photographer Bob Gruen saw the Plasmatics' first performance at The Ritz. "Wendy was captivating, amazing, very sexual," he recalls. "She cut a guitar in half with a buzzsaw. She came out on stage with her nipples covered in black tape crosses. The crowd just loved the band. They'd never seen anything like them. Richie Stotts was wearing a tutu," Gruen remembers, "which was odd – to see a big, solid guy dressed like that. I'd spent a lot of time with The New York Dolls and Arthur "Killer" Kane previously but it was unusual to see a guy looking like that."

"I loved Wendy," says Jean Beauvoir, "She was a great woman. I loved the rebellion she had about her. She was always really kind to me. She was strong willed, she was a great performer, she was all in. Her whole life revolved around rock 'n' roll and the fans. She just gave 100% all the time."

Yet despite Wendy's commanding onstage ferocity, she wasn't the creative force behind her band. The Plasmatics were put together by Rod Swenson – a Yale-educated conceptual artist formerly known as Captain Kink of Captain Kink's Sex Fantasy Theater, a Times Square hybrid of experimental theater and sex show. "I saw that as a laboratory," Swenson told the *Rochester Democrat and Chronicle* in 2016, when the Plasmatics were inducted into the Rochester Music Hall of Fame. Speaking of the 1970s Times Square scene, Swenson said it was a place; "where you could do some very interesting things; experiments in music and visuals and sounds and theatrical performances. It looked like a great place to do some things. Wendy showed up in my life at just the right time, for both of us," Swenson said.

One day in 1976, Wendy O.Williams, who had run away from Webster, NY years earlier at age 16, arrived in New York City at the Port Authority bus terminal. She had spent the previous years drifting through Europe and other parts of the United States, doing odd jobs. After getting off a bus, she walked through the terminal and saw a copy of the *Show Business* newspaper on the floor. A classified ad Swenson placed in that paper looking for performers for Captain Kink's Sex Fantasy Theater caught her eye. She went to a pay phone and called the number in the ad. Swenson answered.

"We were almost done for the day, I was getting ready to leave," Swenson told The *Rochester Democrat and Chronicle* in 2016. "She called and insisted, 'You've got to give me a chance, you've got to see me.' We waited for her. She was just different. She had a small suitcase, everything she had was in it. She had a gold Buddha under her arm, and there was this dancing thing she did, to Jimi Hendrix's 'Foxy Lady,' but with her own voice on this scratchy tape."

Wendy dancing to a tape of *herself* singing "Foxy Lady" is a subversive act – if she danced to Jimi Hendrix singing the song, she would have been just another sex object a man is salivating over. But with *her* singing the lusty lyrics she is observing and praising *her own* sexuality.

"I remember, she emptied her suitcase upside down on the floor and started showing me things," Swenson said to the *Rochester Democrat and Chronicle*, "and she wouldn't stop. It was amazing. I wasn't even sure what to make of it. I said, 'We'll see what we can do.' We put her in for a few days and she just excelled; playing multiple parts, making costumes with me, which she also did for the Plasmatics. She started going with me to rock clubs while I was shooting other things."

Speaking to Phil Sutcliffe in the May 31,1980 issue of *Sounds*, Wendy explained that Captain Kink's Sex Fantasy Theater wasn't typical Times Square sleazy fare:" I will do anything as long as there's a certain *quality* involved," she said." These were like the fucking Cadillacs of sex shows. It was all costumed, choreographed, scripted. This was where I was developing my voice. I was cast as like a dominatrix, a strong female character."

Swenson previously created The Good Shepherd Granola Company (reportedly the first company to successfully market granola in the United States) and was also involved with a New Jersey nudist camp. Circa 1977, in addition to his theater company, Swenson was galvanized by the burgeoning punk rock scene happening in downtown New York. He filmed some videos for bands such as The Ramones and The Dead Boys. Soon he decided to put together a punk rock band, seeking to tap into the iconoclastic energy present in the New York music scene. Rod and Wendy were in the backseat of a taxi when Wendy sang the Bessie Smith song "Sugar In My Bowl" for him. Impressed with the throaty rasp of Wendy's singing voice, he assembled the Plasmatics, with Wendy as the lead singer.

"She was created by Rod but not against her will, nothing underhanded," Ida Langsam says. "I think she was on board with everything. She was kind of wild to begin with. She didn't conform to contemporary morays, yet she was so normal in her personal life. Onstage there was nothing too outrageous for her."

Given that her career was being shaped by a manager like Swenson, that may explain why Wendy isn't regarded as an influence on the Riot Grrrl movement, despite her ferocious femininity. There's no mention of her in *Girls To The Front*, Sara Marcus's book about of that pivotal, feminist, punk-influenced genre that emerged in the 1990s. Bands like Bikini Kill, Bratmobile, Heavens to Betsy, Babes In Toyland,7 Year Bitch and others all consisted (mostly) of young women who wrote their own songs, and played all the instruments in their bands. They booked their own shows and drove their own vans on tour. For the most part, these bands did everything themselves and didn't have management in the traditional sense (at least not management by a man).

Wendy also was not profiled in either edition of *Angry Women*, the RE/Search Publications volumes featuring in-depth interviews with trailblazing women in music such as Bikini Kill singer Kathleen

Hanna, Jarboe from Swans, and Kendra Smith from The Dream Syndicate, among others. "I should have put Wendy O. Williams in my *Angry Women* book!" says V.Vale, co-founder and co-publisher of RE/Search. "I didn't because I thought she was TOO famous! Which she was, at the time—huge mainstream coverage!"

Wendy didn't write the songs she was singing in the Plasmatics – Swenson wrote her lyrics, a substantial part of the band's music and handled the visual aspects as well as business matters for the band. As a performer, and despite being the lead singer of the Plasmatics, Wendy was said to have not been very verbal. Instead she focused more on being physical and was very exhibitionistic. Wendy didn't particularly enjoy giving interviews but as the frontwoman of the Plasmatics and later on during her solo career, she brought a very astute intelligence to discussing the concepts behind her music and performing when she was talking to the press.

In interviews, Wendy often stated her beliefs and sense of purpose regarding what she did onstage in a manner not unlike a political candidate. In the documentary *Wendy O. Williams and the Plasmatics: 10 Years of Revolutionary Rock 'n' Roll,* in a video interview, Wendy says, "I see two different kinds of art: passive art, which goes along with the status quo, and aggressive art which is what we choose – heavy, uncompromising rock 'n' roll." (In keeping with this, the Plasmatics would at times begin their performances by counting off "1-2-Fuck-You!")

"Women on stage are supposed to be almost asexual," Wendy was quoted in an article by Sylvie Simmons in *MOJO*. "It infuriates me," Wendy is quoted as saying. "In front of our shows there's always lots of girls. Girls like having a female out there doing all this stuff and not being inhibited."

Perhaps in line with Wendy's aggressively uninhibited sexual nature and her having performed in a Times Square theater troupe that was part sex show, she was cast in *Candy Goes To Hollywood*, a 1978 adult film. In a scene parodying *The Gong Show*, Wendy performs on "The Dong Show" and shoots ping-pong balls out of her vagina. "Let's see Miley Cyrus do *that*," quipped *Noisey*, in a 2013 article praising Wendy for being a sex-positive maverick among women in music.

Most punk and metal bands of note performed at Trenton, New Jersey venue City Gardens when they made their way along the East Coast. Randy Ellis, who booked the Plasmatics for three performances at the storied venue, recalls Plasmatics fans having a palpable sense of loyalty and reverence for the band "Just like The Ramones did," he says. When the Plasmatics performed, audience members rarely stage dived or attempted to touch Wendy. "She'd come out onstage and it was like 'all hail the queen'", according to Ellis.

Given Wendy's confrontationally sexual demeanor onstage with the Plasmatics, and the sense of devotion among her fans, one wonders if her fans made sexual advances to her that she would take advantage of. Apparently this was not the case. "From what I knew she spent all her time with Rod," says Jean Beauvoir. "We spent quite a lot time together and I know there were pictures of her with Lemmy *(Kilmister, bassist and singer for Motörhead who recorded a cover of "Stand By Your Man" with Wendy)* but she was always with Rod," he says.

"It wasn't easy to get to us because we always had security people to keep people away," Beauvoir continues. "Our fans were very respectful and sexually no one ever really approached us in that way. What we were doing was kind of like a religion for them.

"We always had tight security at the front of the stage, so there was no stage diving. We were always wary of lawsuits so we had good security," says Beauvoir. "No, people were always very respectful of her. She'd speak her mind if they weren't. She could be a little rash and say things but for the most part…she kind of had two sides to her she could be really sweet and gentle but when she got on stage she'd do her thing and be full out."

When asked about whether there were Plasmatics groupies, Plasmatics guitarist Richie Stotts is rather philosophical about the subject: "I have a whole different view of that whole sexual thing with Wendy. I hate when people say – did you fuck her? And they say nasty things but they're missing the whole point of Wendy. My view of Wendy was, it was almost anti-sex. I'm like 'let's grow up.' The people that say that to me and even then… I don't want to sound like a prude because I think there was a lot of sexuality in the band.

There was. She wasn't like Madonna or Debbie Harry or Chrissie Hynde; it was coming at ya right in your face. The whole band was like this. The band was a reflection of the music we played. There was a humorous side to the band and I felt as the band progressed we lost that humor," he says.

"People say "What's the Plasmatics?" Stotts continues. "Now I don't think I have to answer that question, some people in the band have tried to answer that, but when you go ask an artist "what's this painting? Or you ask Jimi Hendrix "What's The Star-Spangled Banner?" I think it's best left unsaid but what I loved most about the band, especially in the early days was that we didn't fit into any category—we weren't a punk band we weren't a metal band--maybe we helped influence something maybe and I think that's true about Wendy… but she had a healthy stable relationship with Rod."

Maria Raha, author of *Cinderella's Big Score: Women of the Punk and Indie Underground*, speaking in the documentary *Wendy O. Williams and the Plasmatics:10 Years of Revolutionary Rock 'n' Roll*, talks about how radical Wendy was in terms of feminism. "Wendy was sexual without being submissive," Raha says. She continues: "A lot of feminism focused on getting a middle-class job; not being assertive and sexually in control as well; enjoying your sexuality. In feminism there was no room for sexuality because people then were afraid of the objectification that came before."
Wendy combined those things, Raha says. "She was able to take the idea of feminism and embrace sexuality and enjoy it as a woman at the same time."

Also in the documentary, Raha states that most women in music were decorative and that the bulk of feminist activity revolved around women finding a place in the middle class – very much maintaining the status quo that Wendy was vehemently out to undermine. "They smiled through a lot of bad shit," Raha says, adding "Wendy had a certain amount of physical aggression and autonomy."

Raha goes on to talk about how Wendy took control of her own sexuality and how the male establishment found that very threatening. "Her view of femininity was not one which subscribed to the idea that to be feminine meant being passive or weak," she says of Wendy in the documentary, adding, "Wendy was very different not only because she wasn't submissive, she was aggressive."

When the Plasmatics emerged, rock music was still very much a male-dominated arena. Really no other woman rock singer was as ferocious a presence on stage as Wendy. She ripped apart conventional notions of what it meant for a woman to be onstage – 300 years before Wendy, women weren't even permitted to play female roles in theater.

Flash forward to the 1960s and many of the most commercially successful women singers were controlled by the men in their lives who viewed them as property, their music and comportment crafted under their male gaze. For example, Sonny Bono bound Cher to an incredibly restrictive contract that prevented her from making records, acting in films and other entertainment types of work when she divorced Bono. (Cher's good friend David Geffen was eventually able to free her from this contract.) Ronnie Spector of The Ronettes was married to producer Phil Spector who had total control of her recording career and her life, really. One day, Ronnie was in the basement of their Beverly Hills home and she saw a coffin. When she asked Spector why it was there, he matter-of-factly told her, "that's the only way you're leaving here." A terrified Ronnie phoned her mother asking her to come get her, and when she did, Ronnie left Spector's home barefoot. At the time of this writing, Ronnie Spector has a substantial solo career where she has been celebrated for her annual performances of Christmas songs. Ronnie sued Phil Spector for royalties that she believed she was owed on Ronettes recordings but she lost the case.

Darlene Love sang on a number of recordings produced by Spector in the Sixties. In a June 2013 interview by David Browne in *Rolling Stone*, Love said of Spector, "We used to tell Phil all the time, 'One of these days, you're going to hurt somebody.'" In 2009, Phil Spector was sentenced to 19 years in prison for murdering actress Lana Clarkson.

In the Seventies, Karen Carpenter was the singer in the internationally famous duo The Carpenters alongside her brother, Richard. They sold millions of records and had several Top Ten hit songs, yet Karen was so miserable she struggled with anorexia and died in her early thirties. The Carpenters' dulcet, ideal-for-Top- 40-radio pop songs were at the far end of the spectrum from the Plasmatics' furious punk-bordering-on-metal sound. There's a sort of irony in the juxtaposition that Wendy was physically much healthier than Carpenter yet she was far from selling millions of records and being as "successful" as her.

Pop superstardom often comes at a price for women yet Wendy's uncompromising nature made it clear that she was not for sale. A July 1980 article by Lynne Farrow in music publication *The Aquarian* bears the headline: "The Plasmatics' Wendy O. Williams, 'Machisma' In Motion." Machisma is a feminized twist on 'machismo" which is defined as a strong sense of masculine pride. Hence machisma – which is not in Merriam Webster's dictionary, though machismo is; one can't help but sense a bit of sexism there -- could be defined as a strong sense of feminine pride, something Wendy exuded. In her article, Farrow writes: "Most women...behave themselves in order to make it. Only *[Wendy O.]* Williams moves to the front lines of feminism with her brand of "machisma," hence her ever-growing female following."

Malcolm Dome, hard rock historian, DJ and former News Editor at *Kerrang!* Magazine, said of Wendy in the *Wendy O. Williams: 10 years of Revolutionary Rock and Roll* documentary: "It doesn't matter that Wendy was male or female in that respect because it was *what she did* that was important. She transcended that whole male/female thing in a way that few artists managed to do. We often hear, 'They're very good for a *girl* band' or 'She's very good for a *female* guitarist.' People stopped saying that when they talked about Wendy because she was very good at what she did – full stop."

Even though Wendy's career was navigated by Rod Swenson, she didn't seem to be his –or anyone's puppet. She and Rod seemed very much to be co-conspirators out to undermine the status quo -- a phrase Wendy and Rod would often say in interviews.

"Conservative male America had castration anxiety when they saw Wendy wielding a chainsaw on TV in the early `80s." says Chris Knowles, writer for *Classic Rock* magazine, in the *Wendy O. Williams and the Plasmatics: 10 years of Revolutionary Rock and Roll* documentary also.

There's a certain paradox in Williams's brazenly sexual onstage persona, the force field she had around herself while performing and how her fans, for the most part, didn't violate her personal space. A video clip of a Plasmatics performance shows Wendy standing in front of a young man in the audience singing to him face -to-face. He is smiling but standing very still. Wendy is topless, wearing little plungers on her nipples and shaving cream smeared on her breasts. At one point Wendy smiles back at the young man, removes one of the mini plungers from her left breast and places it in the young man's hand. He graciously accepts it and doesn't come any closer to Wendy. The tenderness of this gesture is remarkable in light of Wendy's ferocity.

Offstage, Wendy didn't have the out of control personality of a "rock 'n' roll animal," like The Who's hellion drummer Keith Moon or the handful Iggy Pop was during the early '70s. She was known for her politeness and soft-spoken demeanor. "She was kind and she was kind of gentle," says Ida Langsam, "she was so down-to-earth. It was amazing because in person she was so different than the person she was onstage. She was like a different person. It was almost like if she wasn't the performer she was onstage she would have no connection to rock 'n' roll."

When she met with *People* Magazine reporter Carol Wallace to be interviewed at a roadside cafeteria in the Midwest in the early Eighties, Wendy was clad in black leather, a belt that spelled out "Fuck You" in studs and looked, as Wallace puts it, "like a poster girl for the Hell's Angels." A woman on line in front of Wendy wondered aloud where the creamers were. Wendy fetched a handful of them and graciously handed them to the woman.

Wendy left her provocation to the stage. Male shock rock performers of her time often didn't. According to *Trouser Press*, Ozzy Osbourne bit the head off a live dove during a CBS Records marketing meeting. Iggy Pop, known for cutting himself with broken glass onstage and copious drug use, was so troubled and troublesome that he felt the need to remove himself from society. "In 1975 I institutionalized myself voluntarily," Pop told the *Los Angeles Times* in a 1990 article.

Predating Wendy's onstage destruction of television sets there were instances of bands like The Who and The Rolling Stones trashing hotel rooms and throwing television sets out of hotel windows – acts of brattiness born out of schoolboy boredom, making a big splash in the kiddie pool far from the social commentary Wendy was making by smashing a TV onstage (where cleanup was arranged to boot).

When interviewed by Phil Sutcliffe in *Sounds,* Wendy discussed the philosophy behind the Plasmatics:

"The Plasmatics are preserving those feelings you have as an adolescent that you don't fucking know what to do with," she said. "Most people are forced to repress them and they become middle-class. Personally I'd rather be dead than middle-class."

Sutcliffe then asks: "Which 'adolescent' feelings are you talking about? Just finding out you're sexy?"

Wendy replies: "Yeah, but also end-of-the-world feelings, what-am-I-gonna-do feelings, a million things. Paranoia, anger, sometimes you'd like to bomb your parents' house. That's all a part of what we do onstage. Blowing up the Cadillac – it's become like a religion with people to worship material objects and the Plasmatics are showing that these things are just…things. By wrecking them. That's why we could change society."

Wendy had a very radically healthy attitude towards her daily living as well, which was fairly unique for a rock performer in the times she was living in. She was a strict vegetarian who reportedly hated drugs. She didn't smoke or drink alcohol. She was vehemently opposed to refined sugar and insisted that no white bread was served to the band as part of their concert contract rider, instead requesting healthy food items like tofu, bean sprouts and honey. "She taught me about eating healthy, Rod too," Richie Stotts says. "To get rid of bacon, salt, sugar. I still make her hummus and her banana shakes. Nobody was eating like that back then." It has been said that Wendy had an empty Coca-Cola bottle removed from the band's dressing room at a venue because it had "bad karma." Wendy and Rod had an urban garden on the roof of their downtown apartment where they grew wheatgrass.

Wendy exercised daily. She was passionate about lifting weights. Often when she went to a gym to do weight training she was the only woman there. Frequently, she went on six-mile runs. Her body was extremely taut and toned. When she wasn't topless and wearing her trademark black electrical tape on her nipples, she would sometimes appear scantily clad onstage wearing a black bra, skintight black pants or sometimes with electrical tape wound around red pants or just her legs. In a 1979 performance at CBGB, Wendy is wearing a chic strapless red bodysuit with thin blue stripes and matching detached sleeves. This is one of the most modest ensembles Wendy wore onstage (not including television appearances).

Wendy would bend over backwards while singing and hardly stay still while performing. In concert footage of the Plasmatics, Wendy is never out of breath as she runs around the stage. This is most likely due to her being extremely fit.

Wendy's rigorous exercise regime has parallels and differences with Madonna and Gwen Stefani, who, years after Wendy emerged in the public eye, would be celebrated for their commitment to fitness and having bodies in astronomically good shape. Madonna and Stefani are solidly ensconced in mainstream culture and have used their looks and physicality to become brands and make lots of money. Wendy and the Plasmatics took a good portion of their earnings and bought the cars, TVs, guitars etc. to be destroyed onstage and Wendy was always on the cultural fringe.

It's as if Wendy was disciplined for discipline's sake and had no interest in the luxuries that could come from being a commercially successful rock goddess. When the celebrity-driven fitness craze emerged in the Eighties, Wendy didn't cash in with an exercise video or healthy-eating cookbook, though the possibility of her doing so might seem plausible. As she railed against materialism by destroying big- ticket items, the idea of Wendy merchandising her image and personality in a realm outside of music and performing just doesn't quite fit. Using her fame to become a lifestyle brand by manufacturing *things* with her name and/or image on them would seem to run counter to what Wendy stood for.

Wendy was the first woman performer in rock music to wear her hair in a Mohawk. At times it would be all blonde, other times the prominent middle would be dyed black or the sides would be her natural brown. Wendy had been wanting to have a Mohawk for some time before having her hair cut in one circa 1980. Reportedly she wanted to wait until the Plasmatics had gotten substantial notoriety, thus her radical hairstyle would have more impact.

"You have all these cosmetic companies dictating to you what you're supposed to look like, how you're supposed to act," Wendy said in an interview in the documentary *Wendy O. Williams: 10 Years of Revolutionary Rock and Roll*, adding "this is just consensus programming. This is one reason why I cut my hair like this. I'm saying 'fuck you' to all the cosmetic companies."

In Wendy's 1983 interview with *People*, reporter Carol Wallace wrote that Wendy didn't own a place to live and preferred to move from sublet to sublet in downtown Manhattan with just a few possessions; namely foam rubber padding that she would sleep on and a hot plate for cooking. "I'm more interested in having a place to work out my voice and my body than I am in having furniture," she told Wallace, who also reported that Wendy didn't have a phone (the interview took place a good 20-plus years before the ubiquity of smart phones), to which Wendy remarked: "There isn't anybody I want to talk to who I can't see."

"Wendy was a sweet girl, most of the time. I had no issues with Wendy," Stu Deutsch, original drummer for the Plasmatics says, "When I first joined the band in the auditions it was just Richie and Chosei and me. I was called back three or four times and Wendy was at the last audition and it was between me and another guy and I got it.

"So I come into rehearsal one day," Deutsch says, "and Wendy asked, 'Do you want to know the name of the band?' and I had never asked. I surmised that it was going to be Wendy and the something. So I say "Sure" and she says "The Plasmatics," and thought, ok, interesting name. So that was one of my first interactions with Wendy was her telling me the name of the band."

But ultimately, Wendy walked away from rock stardom in the late Eighties after the Plasmatics broke up and after going solo with a band called W.O.W. whose debut album was produced by Gene

Simmons of KISS. Wendy was nominated for a Best Female Rock Vocal Grammy Award for this album in 1985 but lost to Tina Turner. Swenson took a lecturer's position at the University of Connecticut and the two of them moved to the town of Storrs in that state. Wendy volunteered at a health food co-op and did animal rehabilitation, mainly working with squirrels. She had stopped doing any sort of performing or music.

April 6, 1998, a Monday, late afternoon in Storrs, Connecticut—in the woods, birds and squirrels mill about as spring begins to manifest. Rod Swenson comes home to find some objects Wendy left for him: oriental healing balm, a package of buckwheat noodles that he liked, and a note. Swenson reads the note and immediately heads into the woods, looking for Wendy. He finds her - she had just committed suicide by shooting herself, her third and final attempt to end her life.

Had she lived into the 2020s, what would Wendy have thought of our society these days with its omnivorous presence of cell phones and the Internet? Would she have been inspired to perform and smash a giant flat-screen TV or a laptop computer with a sledgehammer?
Or set an iPhone on fire with a blowtorch?

The Plasmatics' song "Living Dead," on their debut album *New Hope For The Wretched,* laments a world of TV-addicted zombies. It's plausible to imagine Wendy railing against those today who live their entire lives online and through their "smart" phones.

The surveillance culture we currently live in – everything from people eagerly revealing intimate details about themselves on social media, to in-home devices such as the Alexa that listen to their owners' conversations and suggest things to buy – might have inspired Wendy to rage against such machines in an even harder manner than the era in which she destroyed cars, televisions, and guitars in the years before privacy eroded away so much.

In 1987, Wendy and a reconstituted line up of the Plasmatics recorded the *Maggots* album, about global warming bringing about the end of society. In the time of *Maggots'* release, global warming (also known as the greenhouse effect) wasn't common knowledge. The album didn't get a lot of attention --it took more than 20 years later for footage of melting icebergs regularly appearing on nightly newscasts to make global warming something that people took to the streets and protested.

As I write this, in 2020, the world is in the grip of the Coronavirus pandemic. Hundreds of thousands of people have died in the United States alone and many people all over the world are sick. Schools and all sorts of businesses are closed and once bustling cities are ghost towns. Had Wendy lived 20 years past the millennium, it wouldn't have been surprising if she intuited such a catastrophic outbreak. Would she have tried to warn us? Would the world have listened?

What made this woman –a woman who was so very much alive, who was so vigilant about how she nourished her body, who pushed herself to extreme physical fitness and had such a passionate life force – want to die? Maybe Wendy just gave up on a world that wouldn't listen to her.

"Wendy felt things so deeply that she couldn't be passive or stand by on the sidelines," Rod Swenson said to *Killdren* magazine in 2008, "she had to be doing."

In an interview with the Rochester, New York *City Paper* in 2016, Rod Swenson said that on the first night he spent with Wendy she talked about why she ran away from home. "The first night that we spent together, she spelled it out for me," Swenson said. "She viewed herself as coming from a small town where she felt very out of place. She wanted to wear different clothes, she wanted to do things differently. She had issues at home and at school. When she left, she was heading out into a world with very few resources and zero contacts. It was a very heroic thing to do. She's not the only person who did that. But in her circumstances, it was very heroic and very courageous, how basically what she wanted was to live an authentic life, without knowing what it is, life."

Wendy once stated: "I'd rather be dead than be brainwashed into the complacent robot everybody wanted me to be."

Wendy From Webster, NY

Wendy Orlean Williams was born on May 28, 1949 in Rochester, NY, to her parents: Audrey Stauber Williams and her husband, Robert Franklin Williams, Jr.

Wendy's parents were married on January 5, 1944. Audrey Stauber Williams, Wendy's mother, grew up in the New York City borough of Queens. Wendy's father, Robert Franklin Williams Jr. was from Alabama and worked as a chemist at Eastman Kodak in Tennessee in the 1930s, eventually relocating to Rochester, where the company was headquartered. During his career at Eastman Kodak, Wendy's father applied for several patents and was granted at least one: Patent number 4119479 for the manufacture of laminates which are useful as packing materials.

In the Williamses' children's birth order, Wendy was the middle child between her two sisters: Barbara, the eldest and Penny, the youngest. Wendy was born on a Saturday and she and her younger sister share a birthday as Penny was born on May 28, 1960. Wendy's birth on this date placed her under the astrological sign of Gemini, whose traits include being passionate, fun loving, easygoing and enjoying being the center of attention. The May birthstone is emerald.

On the day Wendy was born, *The New York Times* reported on Emperor Hirohito of Japan visiting Nagasaki. The cover image of *The New Yorker* on this date was a drawing by Ludwig Bemelmans of a busy Hudson River dock. A year after Wendy was born, Lou Gramm, lead singer for multi-platinum arena rock band Foreigner was born in Rochester as well, though it is not known if he and Wendy crossed paths.

The Williams family lived in Webster, NY--a suburb of Rochester. Webster is on the northeast corner of Monroe County, New York and is named after orator and statesman Daniel Webster. It is bordered on the north by Lake Ontario, on the east by Wayne County, on the west by Irondequoit Bay and the town of Irondequoit and on the south by the town of Penfield. The town of Webster's motto is "Where Life Is Worth Living."

Wendy and her family lived in a brick Cape Cod-style house at 1340 State Road in Webster. Cape Cod houses are typically single-story frame buildings with somewhat steep gabled roofs, a central chimney and hardly any additional decoration. In 1953, the year Wendy's parents bought this house, a local newspaper ad from the John H. Apetz Realty Company lists an asking price of $12,990 for the house, referring to it as one of the "Best Buys of the Week." The Williamses' house had 3 bedrooms and 2 ½ bathrooms. The home was on an acre of treed grounds, had a screened porch, a large family room, a one-car garage, a first-floor laundry room, an eat-in kitchen and a formal dining room with two corner china cupboards.

When Wendy was seven years old, she won a tap dancing contest that lead to an appearance on *The Howdy Doody Show*. A talented clarinet player in middle school, Wendy won a scholarship to study clarinet in a six-month program at the prestigious Eastman School of Music in Rochester.

"I was an outcast, a loner," Wendy told Carol Wallace from *People* magazine in 1983. Wallace reported that "children made fun of her hand-me-down clothes and birdlike figure."

According to *People*, at one point Wendy hosted a party at her home. Children were picking teams for a scavenger hunt and Wendy was in the corner crying because no one included her in their teams.

Wendy felt a sense of betrayal and alienation from her family and home. This was exacerbated when she found out that her beloved dog, Butch, who had disappeared, had in fact been put to sleep by her parents. Throughout her life Wendy was a fervent animal lover. As she told Carol Wallace from *People*: "The thing about animals is that they don't judge you. They accept you the way you are."

Ronald Nesbitt, who was Webster Town Supervisor in 2019, was a classmate of Wendy's at R.L. Thomas High School "I was in a few classes with Wendy back then," he said in an interview for this book, "and I remember her as a shy, soft spoken girl always in the back of the class because her name ended in W." Wendy has often been described as having been a quiet student who paid attention to her appearance and clothing and spoke very softly.

"She was the meekest little lamb you would ever want to know," stated George Hugel, a guidance counselor at R.L. Thomas High, when talking to *People* magazine in 1983. Wendy often felt tormented by her popular, accomplished older sister. An article in the November 27, 1963 *Webster Herald* states that Barbara received six hours of English credit from the University of Kansas towards her Freshman year by completing an Advanced Placement course.

Children tend to be very emotionally invested in their birthdays and one could imagine Wendy feeling a certain sense of being robbed of her "special day" given that her younger sister Penny had the same birthday that she did. Wendy also was alienated from her parents, who she described to *People* as "cocktail zombies," who wanted her to get a 9-to-5 job. Her parents' drinking has been connected to Wendy's refusal to drink alcohol.

As Rod Swenson told *Killdren* magazine, "Part of the early beef with her parents was that she disturbed them by playing loud and "unbecoming" rock music in her room and that drove them crazy."

Hints of Wendy's wild side emerged in her early teens. She was kicked out of the Girl Scouts for flirting with boys on a canoe trip. At 15, she was arrested for nude sunbathing at Letchworth State Park, near Rochester. When she showed up for her first day of work at B. Forman's department store, she was sent home because her skirt was too short.

In her sophomore year at R.L. Thomas High School, Wendy bleached her brown hair blonde and stayed away from home for nights on end. She lost her virginity to a man she met at a bar. "For me that was sex," she told Wallace from *People*. "If you were supposed to do one thing, I did the other just because I didn't know what to do."

According to a statement by Wendy's childhood friend Suzanne Albright in an April 25, 2016 *Rochester Democrat and Chronicle* article written by Jeff Spevak, Wendy was married at age 16 to a man who was in the Navy. According to Albright, who claimed to be a witness at the wedding, the ceremony took place at St. Matthias Episcopal Church in East Rochester. The couple moved to South Carolina but the marriage ended quickly.

Wendy ran away from Webster when she was 16. She hitchhiked to Colorado with a small amount of money from her part time job at Dunkin' Donuts, lived in a tent outside of Boulder where she sold string bikinis and macramé. In Florida she slept on the beach and was a lifeguard and sailing instructor. Making her way to Europe, she tended bar in Amsterdam, was a cook in a macrobiotic restaurant in London and was a dancer in a gypsy troupe. She was arrested for shoplifting once and on another occasion for passing counterfeit money.

In 1965, the year Wendy left home, Wendy's mother placed an ad in the classifieds of the Rochester *Democrat and Chronicle* selling her mink coat. In interviews later on, Wendy would say that she came from "Anytown, Anywhere."

Peter Morticelli dated Wendy when she returned for a while to the Western part of New York State in 1970. As he recalls, that summer Wendy was waitressing at a steakhouse restaurant in a vacation spot on a small lake. Peter was in a band called Hardware that was enjoying some popularity in the region.

One night, Morticelli went to the restaurant where Wendy was working to see a friend's band who were playing there. "I noticed that there was a waitress there who was a knockout," Morticelli says, "A beautiful face, a petite, athletic body; curly, platinum blondee hair (not natural but very cool looking). We talked quite a bit that night. We even played a game that was in the bar. It was a shuffleboard type game that involved metal disks sliding down what looked like a miniature bowling alley with sawdust on it to help the disks slide better. She was taking a lot of time away from the customers to talk with me. A lot of that was my fault because I kept engaging her in conversation. I was pretty sure that if this continued, she would get fired and I definitely didn't want to see that happen. So, we made plans to see each other after she was done with work. I was completely taken with her, no two ways about it. I was ready to spend a lot more time with her."

As to what attracted Morticelli to Wendy, he explains that she made her waitress uniform into a very sexy "costume" and he liked how soft-spoken she was. "The more we talked, the more I was impressed by her," Morticelli says, "She was no airhead that was certain. She seemed very spiritual. It was obvious that she had given a lot of thought to various subjects. Honestly, these were subjects that were not things that I cared much about. I never was able to get into a lot of the stuff that she tried to introduce me to."

Often Wendy would give Morticelli small gifts: books of poetry and writing by Kahlil Gibran, little figurines or framed photographs of small animals and birds. He and Wendy saw each other as often as they could over the next few weeks but conflicting work schedules and logistical problems hampered their relationship. "My place was a lot closer to her job. So, that was convenient for her," says Morticelli, "But it didn't always work out because some nights I wasn't returning there at all or until 5 or 6 in the morning due to our playing schedule.

"The one thing that I knew for sure was that although she liked music and she liked bands and band members, I never once got the impression that she wanted to become a singer or a performer of any type," he says.

Morticelli recalls an instance that foreshadowed Wendy's predilection for provocative comportment: "I remember that Hardware was playing a club in Rochester. She told me that she would be able to attend that show. We were already into our first set and were going over very well with the crowd when she arrived. Her entrance was electric. The entire place went nuclear. Wendy strolled in wearing a brand new, pure white, men's t-shirt (Size Large so that it became a very short mini-dress), white tennis/deck shoes and that's all. My vague recollection is that she attracted so much attention it became impossible for her to stay. I hated to see her go but it was probably in the best interests of everyone there."

The restaurant Wendy worked at was only open seasonally and closed at the end of August. "It became hard work to coordinate our schedules and it was almost easier not to see each other," Morticelli says, "but I did everything I could to keep it going. I really wanted to keep it going because she was so special to me.

"In the end, I just stopped hearing from her," he says. "That was it. I always felt that maybe I wasn't 'exciting' enough for her. I didn't drink, I didn't do drugs. I was really focused on my interests and they were different interests than hers (or, so I thought). That was the end of a few months with Wendy."

Morticelli did run into Wendy again about two years later, as he explains: "I was walking through a suburban shopping mall east of Rochester when Wendy emerged from a health food store. Apparently, she worked there. We had a conversation during which I told her that I had gotten married. She got an angry expression on her face, told me I was "stupid" and walked away. I never saw or heard from her again."

In the early `80s, Morticelli was managing rock bands. One of them, a metal band called The Rods – played a show in New York on a bill with the Plasmatics. Unaware that the singer for the Plasmatics was Wendy, Morticelli instead went to see one of the other bands he was working with that night. "When I talked to the Rods the day after the show," he says, "they told me about the Plasmatics' show and how wild their singer was. They asked me if I knew her. They told me that her name was Wendy O. and that she was from Rochester. It didn't resonate with me. But I was interested to find out more about this singer from Rochester. I don't really know how I finally figured out that Wendy O. was really Wendy Williams from Webster, NY. I was shocked beyond shocked. On one hand I regretted not attending that show. On the other hand, I don't think I would have known what to do or what to say to Wendy. Some kind of monumental transformation had occurred for her over a period of 10 or 12 years. I have no idea how any of it came to be. This was not the same person that I knew and cared about. She was on her own path now and I apparently could only play catch up."

"She was a 'star' of sorts," Morticelli reflects, "I was happy for her. Although we were both involved in the music business, we never ran across one another. She might have been as oblivious to me and my activities as I was of hers. And that was probably for the better."

(Aside from managing bands, Morticelli has been active in the music

34

industry over the years. He created a subscription-based company that delivered live concerts over the Internet by The Allman Brothers during their 40th anniversary year. He also started Magna Carta Records, a boutique label specializing in progressive heavy metal. Well-regarded for the virtuosity of its artists, Magna Carta was successful and Morticelli sold the label in 2018.)

Wendy returned to Rochester in 1983 when the Plasmatics played a concert at Harmonia Gardens, a venue under a tent in the parking lot of the Red Creek Inn club on June 11 of that year. When talking to Andy Smith from the *Rochester Democrat and Chronicle* a week before the show, Wendy said: "I don't know of any woman who sings rock 'n' roll the way I do. There's nothing dainty about me. I spill my guts on stage – but I don't do anything a male rock singer doesn't do. I hate the role images people get – that there's something wrong with you if you don't look like the Revlon girl. I've never looked like the Revlon girl."

Ladies and Gentlemen – the Plasmatics

Somewhat akin to how Wendy left Webster, NY when she was 16 in search of a life where she felt a greater sense of meaning, Richie Stotts dropped out of the State University of New York at Fredonia in 1974 and moved to New York City. Traveling with artist friend Michael David, and with his imagination ignited by the MC5, Frank Zappa's Mothers of Invention and other bands ranging from The Stooges to the Grateful Dead, Richie knew he wanted to be a musician.

Following his instincts once he got to Manhattan, Stotts started going to a biker bar on Bowery that would soon be the focal point of a musical revolution. "Hilly used to say to me `You were the second customer at CBGB,' because I went there before the music was there," Stotts says in 2019, sitting for an interview in a Greenwich Village diner. "I had a girlfriend who lived on Horatio Street, Richard Lloyd *[guitarist for the bands The Heartbreakers and Television]* lived above me – he got me an audition with the Heartbreakers," Stotts recalls.

In the Downtown Manhattan of the mid-Seventies, there was no gold-rush clamor to be a rock star like there is in the hyper-gentrified, everyone-in-Brooklyn-is –in-a-band New York of the time of my interview with Richie Stotts. According to Stotts, back during the days of New York's fiscal crisis coupled with a huge crime rate when everyone was broke, he wanted to pursue music but there was no pre-set way to go about it. "Nobody went out to bars because nobody had any money," he said. "Nowadays 20 year- old kids are buying 10 and 15 dollar martinis. We were just drinking Budweiser."

In this atmosphere of urban blight that would soon sprout an earthshaking music scene growing out of CBGB, Stotts and friend Michael David played together in a band called Numbers ("Michael David's still an artist in Bushwick now," Stotts said in our interview). At this time Stotts was becoming aware of the New York Dolls and David Bowie. As he recalls, "There was no more Rolling Stones, they were too big and the whole '70s thing – that was the context of the punk thing -- no one could just get onstage and be Led Zeppelin – although I love Led Zeppelin now but at the time it was like an unattainable thing."

Stotts didn't join The Heartbreakers but played guitar in Numbers and had a French manager who told him to get rid of his Stratocaster and Ampeg amp and go with the sound of a Les Paul guitar and a Marshall amp. He was living with Michael David on Bond Street between Bowery and Broadway; walking distance to CBGB where Stotts snuck in to see The Ramones. He saw Television several times during their fabled Sunday night residency there and he was often in the audience when Patti Smith alchemized rock 'n' roll and poetry accompanied by just Lenny Kaye on guitar.

In our 2019 interview, decades after the Plasmatics split up, Stotts is a long way from his flying vee guitar-wielding, blue Mohawk hairstyle-wearing days; he's working in the computer field, married and very "normal." Surprisingly, when a worker at the diner where I interviewed him slammed a bus tray full of dishes and glasses into a waiter's station shelf behind Stotts, making a loud, clattering burst of noise right behind him, Stotts cringed in discomfort. Clearly his years of playing high-decibel guitar that walked the screeching tightrope between punk and metal are in his past.

"I think everything has to be…you gotta look at the whole time period, the historical context of the band, what was happening, who I was," Stotts says. "I met Rod and Wendy in 1977. I wanted to come down here because I wanted to be a musician. As a kid I loved the blues but also rock 'n' roll too. I had a shag haircut coming down from upstate NY and I was a part Deadhead and a part blues fan, part Mothers of Invention, Iggy Stooge…one of my favorite bands was the MC5 – I think I discovered them. I got their first album when I was in a store called Caldor's with my mom and I slipped it in her bag. I wrote to the White Panthers. About ten/20 years later I saw Wayne Kramer in a hardware store and he recognized me and I said "shit, I got your album," and then I played with him a couple of years ago."

"I was coming down here not knowing what I was gonna...I wanted to be a musician," Stotts says." I liked the blues but I also liked rock, more like the MC5 type of thing. And when I came down here there was the New York Dolls and I didn't know what the hell that was."

New York City in the days when Stotts had just moved there was a markedly different landscape from how it was in 2019 during our conversation. In the mid-Seventies, Richie was living in a loft that rented for a mere $300 a month in the neighborhood that eventually became branded as NoHo (meaning North of Houston Street). In 2019 "loft-style" apartments in NoHo currently have six-figure and higher selling prices. When Richie lived on Bond Street and his band Numbers was booked at CBGB he could easily wheel his amplifier three blocks to the club. "I was playing with Michael David and this drummer, Roy Stuart --now he's a famous photographer who's been published by Taschen Books. But back then people had lofts. Lofts were cheap," Stotts says. "I was living at One Bond Street. Go down check it out it's a beautiful building. There were three of us living there, my rent was $95 a month. I had a little room – it was a giant space."

"But here's another thing, "Stotts says with a tone of foreboding, "if you went east of Broadway it was *dangerous*. There was none of this stuff like now. People talk about Alphabet City? Forget about it- east of Broadway was bad. Nowadays everybody thinks it's such a hip area. It was a dump. I lived for 14 years on the Lower East Side on Suffolk Street. It was a dump then and it's still a dump."

At this time when Stotts was trying to find his place in the nascent Downtown music scene he still had to pay that $95 rent. "I had a bunch of crazy jobs," Stotts continues. He sold knife sets on the street and got a job as a music copyist with one Arnold Arnstein - the foremost name in the music copying field. "Copying is when a composer writes a score for an opera or a musical and on each line is an instrument," as Stotts explained, "and the music copyist's job is to extract each part out as a separate part; not only that, you have to do editing – a good copyist knows 'this part is out of range for a flute," you copy each part out. He was the big shot." Stotts got in touch with Arnstein back then the old-fashioned way – by looking him up in the phone directory. "I just looked him up and he was the chief copyist for *West Side Story*, he worked with Leonard Bernstein, he worked with Charles Mingus – jazz guys, the heavy classical people. I had a little bit of a "music background" so I felt I could do this, and I felt like instead of hustling knives and stuff that I could be in the music business."

"So I'm doing this job," Stotts continues "and I have this band and Roy, our drummer, he was like the connected guy in the music business, he worked at the Show World theater on 42nd Street, a bunch of people worked there like Patti Smith's guitar player or something, people like that. Roy said 'when we get good enough we can bring Rod Swenson down to see the band – typical music kinda 'I've got a connection,' you know what I'm saying. So we practice and practice, there were 3, maybe four of us and we said 'Roy when might this Rod Swenson guy be willing to come down to see the band?' and he says, "We gotta get better."

   As Stotts tells it, music venues were scarce back then. "There were only two places to play: CBGB and Max's Kansas City. Nowadays there's a million places to play! You could probably go over to *[Sixth Avenue hot dog stand]* Papaya Dog and convince them to book you," he says without any irony. "…and you can play on the street now and make a little money but back then there were just these two places."

   As Stotts describes the downtown Manhattan music scene in the early-to-mid Seventies, it was far from the careerist milieu it had become at the time of our conversation. As he puts it, there was a certain guileless quality in the air. "Nobody really knew what was happening," Stotts says of the CBGB/ Max's Kansas City Scene back then. "Some of my friends who were a bit more in tune with what was happening in New York would say 'Oh, Clive Davis is over there,' people were showing up but it wasn't crowded then, right at the beginning. Something was happening but I didn't know what was happening. Then it sort of took off."

But things were also happening in the lofts that were plentiful and affordable, as Stotts explains: "What happened is we did this gig. Jean Beauvoir was in a band called the New York Niggers. And I had another friend, Leo, and another guy was in it they had a loft on Greenwich Street."

"So we played this loft the NYN had," he explains, "and Rod came to the show and brought Wendy with him. I didn't meet either of them. We did the show and I said, "What did Rod say? What did he think of the band?" Roy said, 'Oh, I'm working with him, I'm working with some songs." So consider that I at least wrote part of every song I was getting a little concerned because I was saying, what's really going on here? Roy wasn't really that much of a songwriter. He's a good drummer but he wasn't writing songs. We rehearsed in his loft up in the Garment District. And Michael had his art thing going on."

Stotts wanted to get in touch with this well-regarded Rod Swenson himself, so he did what he did when he wanted a job with Arnold Arnstein: "I got the phone book out and I looked up Rod Swenson and I just called him up and we started talking," Stotts says, "and I said I wrote most of the songs for the band I was in or at least part of them and I'm involved in this whole thing and he said, 'How soon can you come down here?' He was down on Thomas Street in TriBeCa and I was on Bedford Street in the heyday of the whole gay/Greenwich Village scene. It was packed on weekends, people were going to the piers, it was like Woodstock every day. That's a thing to understand about the city then. Things were freer than they are now."

Stotts knew he needed to talk to Rod Swenson, so he went to see him: "I went down to talk to Rod and he thought Roy was the songwriter, I'm working on songs and then I listen to the songs and they're nothing that we did."

"I think I went down with my guitar another time," Stotts says. He and Swenson talked and Swenson said "This is the story, I want to start a rock band, manage a rock band." As Stotts recalls, Swenson was dabbling in managing with a band from Toronto called The Diodes and he was shooting video of CB's bands like the Ramones and The Dead Boys. "But he told me," Stotts says "that his vision of the band was to have a rock band with Wendy as the singer. And he says 'Wendy doesn't have any experience singing but I believe she can be a great performer because of the work I've done with her. '"

At this point Stotts was still sporting an early-Seventies shag haircut. He was 24 years old and, as he put it: "I'm already feeling old in this business, so I'm like, ok." Rod says "I need someone who can help me put a band together, what I need is somebody who can write the music, I'll write the lyrics, I'll worry about Wendy if you can put the band together and write the songs. I've got a little money so we can go into the studio and record," and I'm like…I felt a little bit about my friends in The Numbers, he felt that they could audition but "you're in – I'll give you the shot if you can do this." That's how the band started."

Stotts lived near original Plasmatics bassist Chosei Funahara in the West Village and he thought Funahara would be a suitable member of this nascent band, partly because, as Stotts put it: "He had a really cool bass and a shaved head. I hadn't seen Wendy perform yet but I had met her. Rod's a smart guy, he's kind of visual person art guy and it kinda fit in to my other side of stuff; I liked Albert King and Muddy Waters – those guys were great showmen; Chuck Berry too but at the same time, The Mothers of Invention and I was a child of the 60s, Rod was eight years my senior but I kinda understood what he was coming from and he was a promoter and he had a funny sense of humor."

"So we got Chosei, we got Stu," Stotts continues, "we met and started in 1977. We rehearsed, Rod wrote the lyrics, worked with Wendy we would work the songs out and Wendy would come in and Rod would lay the vocals on top of the band. That's the beginning of the relationship, the kernel of the band. We didn't have any masterplan of how we would do this so at that first show, we had, I think Rod came up with the idea of "Butcher Baby" we had a song called "Butcher Baby" so Rod said, "Why don't you put on some butcher jackets?" and we got Chosei who's this cool-looking Japanese guy who's in great shape, shaved head and then Wendy comes out and she takes her top off and also the music was so fast and it wasn't the Ramones sound, we kind of had a bluesy, harder sound."

Around the time Plasmatics were building up an audience at CBGB it was decided that they needed to add a second guitar player. An ad in the *Village Voice* was placed seeking the "world's fastest, most precise rhythm guitarist, for world's most extreme rock 'n' roll band." In the *Wendy O. Williams 10 Years Of Revolutionary Rock and Roll* documentary, Wes Beech describes his successful tryout for the band: "I'd seen Wendy and she was totally riveting," he says. "I showed up at the audition and it was like something out of a Fellini movie," he says. "Chosei led me down to a dank, dark basement with dripping pipes. The rest is history."

Original Plasmatics drummer Stu Deutsch recalls: "When I first joined the band in the auditions it was just Richie and Chosei and me. I was called back three or four times and Wendy was at the last audition and it was between me and another guy and I got it. Then we started rehearsing."

"I knew of Rod," Deutsch continues "because he had done these Miss Bare All America pageants at the Beacon Theater– nude contestants and The Dictators were the house band. The Dictators were friends of mine so I got to go to those shows," he says.

According to Stotts, right from the beginning, the Plasmatics were determined to be unlike any typical rock band before them.

"So when we got up on stage it wasn't like 'we're gonna tune our guitars and just sort of jam through," says Stotts. "It was like 'We're coming at ya! We were creating a *show*. One of the things critics and critiques of the band get wrong, they always view it through the lens of a music band but it was… something *else*. Now, I love Broadway shows and opera and all that stuff but we're coming at ya, we're not just getting up there playing songs – this is a whole visual thing."

As CBGB owner Hilly Kristal stated in an interview segment on the *Wendy O. Williams and the Plasmatics: 10 Years of Revolutionary Rock 'n' Roll* documentary, when talking about Wendy: "Something in her had to be let out. When we talk about passion, Wendy always had the energy and the passion – it was always a great performance."

Soon after their debut at CBGB, word quickly spread about the Plasmatics and they were selling out four nights a week there with fans queuing up for their performances all down the Bowery. Also in the *Wendy O. Williams and the Plasmatics: 10 Years of Revolutionary Rock and Roll* documentary, Wes Beech reflects on the fan base the Plasmatics were building up in their early shows at CBGB: "Oh it was crazy, there were lines down the block," he says. " It was so packed you could hardly get to the stage. It was just totally wild."

Realizing that they were outgrowing the birthplace of punk and needing to play a mid-sized concert site in Manhattan but not finding a suitable one, Swenson approached the Polish war veterans who ran the Irving Place polka hall Irving Plaza. He convinced them to rent the space to him for a reasonable fee, according to the documentary *Wendy O. and the Plasmatics, 10 Years of Revolutionary Rock And Roll.*

But there was a problem – Irving Plaza wasn't a live rock music venue. It did have a stage, good sightlines and a convenient downtown location, but there was no in-house sound system or lighting rig. So Swenson sold his motorcycle and bought the necessary sound and lighting equipment for the Plasmatics to have a concert there.

Also, and this was fairly troubling to Rod and the Plasmatics -- there was no way to arrange for pre-sold tickets to the show; ticket sales had to be done at the box office right before showtime. Doing this was a huge gamble for Swenson and the band members both in terms of their sketchy financial picture at that time and the band's reputation. Selling out CBGB, a club that had a 350 capacity, on a steady basis was one thing --CBGB had such cachet that it was entirely possible that some audience members at Plasmatics shows were there just because they wanted to make the scene at the famous punk rock club, regardless of who was performing. But playing a much bigger hall, with a 1200 capacity— over three times as many people as CBGB without any advance ticket sales … what if nobody came to the show?

Fortunately for the band, the Plasmatics' Irving Plaza debut in December of 1978 was a triumph. Despite a steady rain falling all day, word of mouth was so strong that a huge mass of devoted umbrella-toting fans lined up around the Irving Place block to get into the show. There's a photo in the *Wendy O. Williams and the*

Plasmatics: 10 Years of Revolutionary Rock and Roll documentary of a large group of Plasmatics fans assembled outside the venue's front doors that day, waiting to buy tickets and holding up their middle fingers *en masse* to the camera. The tickets for the show sold out and the venue was filled to capacity, with many fans being turned away. the Plasmatics were a smash success that night and would soon appear on the cover of the *SoHo Weekly News*. That Plasmatics concert christened Irving Plaza as a New York live rock music venue. Throughout the Eighties and into the early 2000s, what had had just been a barely used polka hall thrived as a New York City rock music concert hall, hosting top-name acts in the Alternative genre such as U2, Gang of Four, Beck, The Jesus Lizard, Sonic Youth, Urge Overkill, Placebo, The Old 97s, the re-formed New York Dolls, among many others.

Dynamics between band members are a key element of any rock group. If there's conflict or tension that just won't go away that usually sets the clock ticking on how long a band will be recording and performing together. It's not accurate to describe the members of the Plasmatics as friends picking up instruments in pursuit of creative fun in a "Hey, let's put on a show," manner. They were very much a businesslike organization.

"My relationship with Wendy was a complicated one, a complicated one," says Richie Stotts "I don't want to say it was a professional relationship but it was," he says of how he got along with Wendy. "In a way she was like my sister; we all took our clothes off and got dressed together in these little tiny rooms. One time Wendy got really mad at me and she hit me and we would knock over amps onstage. I have a friend who says what we were doing was like professional wrestling – is it real or is it not? Wendy shot me with a shotgun loaded with blanks once. I still have the scar on my leg.

"There was a lot of stuff that was dangerous," he continues, talking about the destruction taking place at Plasmatics concerts. "I knocked some amps over on her at the Heat Club *[a TriBeCa nightspot at that time]*I didn't mean to-- and she had a photo shoot the next day and she got upset but we made up. That's the only time during the band I had any issue with Wendy. Our show was so amazing--the stage would be dark and then a video would come on and the dry ice would come on, Wendy would bang something then it would be like 1,2,3,4 and it just exploded."

According to Jean Beauvoir, the Plasmatics were a very diligent, organized, hardworking rock band who took blowing up cars, speakers etc. as seriously as they approached their music – they had to for their own safety. He says they were very precise: "The band was involved in how things were being done. We'd say: 'we're going to shoot the speakers at that time, we need a certain amount of music for that.' We'd rehearse all the time, we were a 9to5 rock band, five days a week every week. We'd spend most of our time going through the show from beginning to end because everything had to be perfectly timed so no one would get killed."

In rock 'n' roll lore, the automobile is an object of desire – one that's sung about and praised by musicians ranging from Chuck Berry to Bruce Springsteen to George Thorogood and more. But the Plasmatics viewed the automobile – specifically the Cadillac, America's favorite luxury car – as a consumer culture fetish object to destroy as part of their performances. "We'd research Cadillacs, drive around in them for a while, get other stuff and just do it," says Jean Beauvoir.

When the Plasmatics were booked at The Palladium in November of 1979, they were the first band without a record deal to sell out the venue – and the only band anywhere whose show featured an exploding Cadillac.

"The first time we blew up a car was at The Palladium," says Richie Stotts. "How we would do it was we'd get a guy to cut the car up into quarters or eighths and put it back together so when the car blew up it would fly away but not too far. Somebody forgot to tie down the hood. Now The Palladium was a huge theater – one of these old fashioned monsters, it looked like *Phantom of the Opera* there. We blew up the car and all of a sudden it blew up the speakers and our guitars – it sounded like *Saving Private Ryan* and all of a sudden out of the smoke this hood comes crashing down. If it landed in the audience it would have killed someone. It was dangerous what we were doing – really dangerous."

"They got me a motorcycle helmet," says Stu Deutsch, drummer for the Plasmatics at the Palladium show, where the band first blew up a Cadillac, "and one of the pyro guys said, 'Yeah, you wear it as protection – if you get decapitated your head will still be in one piece,' something ridiculous like that. I was the closest to it. The guitarists can get off stage but I gotta stay there behind the kit." (Fortunately for Deutsch, he survived the blowing up of the Cadillac on stage at The Palladium and lived to tell the tale during an interview in 2019.)

Mark Smethurst, a doctor who was a teenager in New York City in the late Seventies, saw the Plasmatics at that Palladium concert when he was 15. "I had heard about the Plasmatics from the punk crowd at Stuyvesant High School," he says. "The show was on November 16, 1979. I remember Mitch Ryder and the Detroit Wheels opened. I hated Mitch Ryder because it was this rah-rah Bruce Springsteen rock 'n' roll which I never liked. That bored me to tears."

Smethurst wasn't the only audience member who disliked Ryder that night. Music journalist Roy Trakin, writing in the *New York Rocker* claimed that Ryder was "booed off the stage by some of the more ravenously depraved members of the crowd."

"There was an incredibly long break between sets. So the video for the Plasmatics' song "Fast Food Service" plays on the big screen," Smethurst continues, "then the screen goes up and the stage is dark. There are three TV sets in the middle of the stage, they all light up, playing static and Wendy O. comes out with the lights off and smashes the television sets in turn with a sledgehammer and the middle set was the last one she smashed and when she smashed the last one, the lights came on and the band was on stage and they started."

According to Smethurst, Wendy started the show topless with electrical tape on her nipples and at one point changed into a fishnet cat suit. In filmed footage of the show, Wendy's blonde hair hangs down her back in a long braid and she's wearing protective earphones during the sequence where the Cadillac blows up. Richie Stotts sported a blue Mohawk, a tutu and combat boots. He played a guitar shaped like a parallelogram. At the end of the first set, Wendy cut up an electric guitar with a chainsaw.

"Wendy really used the entire stage," Smethurst continues, "she was moving around to the ends and the middle, working the crowd, in the front a lot. She had a microphone on a long cord, nothing was radio then. They had a set break. I don't think the Cadillac was there at the beginning, I think they moved it onto the stage for the second half. I was looking forward to seeing the Cadillac blow up. It's hard to say that I was scared. I was a teenage pyro so if she hadn't done it I would have thought of it. It was really impressive to my adolescent sensibility of 'destroy this symbol.' I only had one relative who had a Cadillac."

Mark Smethurst found Wendy sexually provocative onstage and it had an unusual effect on him as a young teenage boy: "Because of my exposure to sex shows like *Midnight Blue* on Manhattan Cable Television, the vibe and the moves weren't that unfamiliar but she was aggressive about it, she was in your face about it, and she did it over and over in time with the music in a creative way, reaching out to band members and audience members with the simulating masturbation on stage."

He continues: "It got to be where even for a 15 year-old I was uncomfortable but it felt *right* that I was uncomfortable. It was clearly intentional, so it broke through whatever adolescent titillation I might have gotten out of seeing someone with a body like hers, practically naked being very sexual. It was like, 'no you don't get to get off on this,' but at the same time how can you not?"

"I don't much care for the Plasmatics," Roy Trakin stated his *New York Rocker* review of the Palladium show, "but Rod Swenson has got his fingers on the pulse even if his thumb is squarely up the ass of the captive American consumer." Also in *the New York Rocker*, Trakin summarily stated, when speaking of the Plasmatics' Palladium concert: "As I sat in the fourth row, contemplating whether I'd get a bumper in my mouth, the destruction of the Cadillac was accomplished with impressive professionalism..." he then talks about how "the beleaguered Coupe de Ville...heaved and coughed and finally died taking 2000 years of civilization with it."

At a later Plasmatics performance, during the song "Corruption," Wendy is clad in her leopard print frontless jumpsuit, black tape on her nipples and splashes of bright pink in her platinum blonde hair.

An orange hot rod with a wide black stripe down the front hood, possibly a Mustang, was onstage destined to be destroyed. Wendy smashed the windshield and placed explosives in the car three separate times. The first two explosions didn't do too much damage. Upon tossing the last stick of dynamite with a lit fuse through the passenger side window, Wendy gets away from the car. She doesn't seem the least bit scared; she skips as if gleeful. The car blows up in a volcanic rush of skyward flames and Wendy, watching from a safe distance at stage left, thrusts her arms in the air victoriously.

Washington Post reporter Richard Harrington interviewed Wendy in a November 22, 1980 article about the Plasmatics and she said, "People worship 'things.' You work for them and take care of them and these things become your gods. What we do is show that they're just things." Also in the article, Harrington discusses with Wendy how the Plasmatics acquire the things they destroy "Everything works, everything is new,' Williams said. "We call them disposable. We blow up our profits. People ask who pays for them. Our fans pay for them. The more popular we become the bigger our shows will be, the more we'll put into them. This is what gets us off. This is what we're after -- getting off."

By this time, the Plasmatics were getting steady press and the music industry was taking notice. In *Billboard*, Roman Kozak was regularly covering them. At one point he wrote, *"[The Plasmatics make]* Alice Cooper and KISS look like greasy kid stuff." He also called them "Not only the most popular unsigned band in New York, but also the best."

"The Plasmatics are the final solution to rock 'n' roll," Roy Trakin also wrote in the *New York Rocker* review--a very apt description; the Plasmatics were at the far end of the rock spectrum – a vast distance from bands perpetuating the party ethos standard of rock music. Their concerts were more like witnessing a ritual sacrifice seeking to purify a toxic culture than seeing musicians onstage trying to be rock virtuosos encouraging the audience to have a typical good time.

The Plasmatics challenged not only the meaning of rock 'n' roll performance, but they questioned the concept of entertainment itself. There was a quotient of danger in a Plasmatics concert: exploding cars --where would that hood land? Wendy wielding a chainsaw --

what if she wanted to slice apart more than a guitar? What if she goes in to the audience with the chainsaw? A television set being pounded with a sledgehammer – look out for that flying glass! Sure, Alice Cooper put his head through a faux guillotine every night on tour and blood would come out of KISS members' mouths, but those types of antics were just showbiz in the safe confines of theatricality. Going to a Plasmatics concert meant wondering not just what would happen onstage but what would happen to *you*. That's cathartic performance indeed.

Plasmatics fan Jeff Shilling recalls seeing a Plasmatics performance at the Fountain Casino in New Jersey. "I was front row, it was a really good show. Wendy was wearing her leopard print panties, electrical tape and shaving cream. It's getting towards the end of the show and she smashes a TV. This piece of metal goes flying over my head and hits the guy behind me right between the eyes and he's bleeding. People think it's a part of the show but the blood was just pouring out of his face."

"The aura of catastrophe is intriguing to me," Rod Swenson remarked to Phil Sutcliffe in *Sounds*. "I think people come to the Plasmatics with an idea of what they're going to see but when it actually happens they're afraid and for an instant they wish they hadn't come. 'Uhoh, this is it' Y'know. That's a great moment because when it's over they think 'Hey! We made it! We got through!' and they feel good. Our job is to take it to that edge, but control it."

Jack Mulholland, was a member of the Secret Service, the Plasmatics' fan club. He was an ardent fan of the Plasmatics in the late '70s/early '80s.

Mulholland is a former club owner and he's a licensed attorney in the State of New York.

"I owned a rock club called Bluto's in the Catskill Mountains in a little town called Delhi," he says. "There was a two-year state school there and that's why I figured I could be a rock promoter because I had this young, built-in audience that could walk to my club."

Mulholland often traveled to see the Plasmatics whenever he had the opportunity. He saw them twice in Boston; once at the Paradise and later, when he owned Bluto's he was able to go backstage at The

Channel. He then saw them in New York at the Palladium and at Bond's. Mulholland very much wanted to book the Plasmatics at his club.

"I saw the Plasmatics at a club in Albany, New York," Mulholland stated in a 2019 interview. "I don't remember the name of the club but on the marquee they were advertised as 'porn rock.'

In the November 22 1980 article in the *Washington Post,* Wendy expresses her distaste for the term "porn rock." "It infuriates me," said Wendy to reporter Richard Harrington. "Heavy metal punk, okay. Acid punk, okay. But porno rock?"

"This is when I had my first and only really one-on-one conversation with Rod Swenson," said Mulholland in a 2019 interview.

"So prior to the show, everything was set up, the audience was assembling but it was still relatively early," Mulholland recalls. "A little way off to the side of the bar were some tables and Rod was there doing some paperwork. So I went over to Rod because I was very curious given that Wendy's initials spelled W.O.W. I was wondering if her real name was Wendy O. Williams. So I sit down, introduce myself, I tell him that I own a club in the Catskills and that I was interested in booking the Plasmatics in my club and the first question I ask –I was very curious – I ask is Wendy O. Williams her name or a stage name? And he said, 'No, that's her real name.' He was very courteous but he said when I described my club that the Plasmatics would not be able to play there because my ceiling was too low and it was made out of wood and he was afraid the band's pyrotechnics would set the club on fire."

Mulholland saw the Plasmatics at the aforementioned gig at Heat, the TriBeCa club in downtown Manhattan. As he describes it: "It was a very little club but I think that the coziness of the club – it was so small it somehow made for a very unique atmosphere and for some reason it sticks in my mind as the most dynamic and energetic show of theirs that I saw; just seeing Wendy sing the phrase "sometimes I, FEEL IT! about 12 times was mesmerizing."
Oeidipus, the highly regarded DJ on iInfluential Boston radio station WBCN, called the Plasmatics "The most outrageous rock 'n' roll band in the world."

The first time the Plasmatics played at City Gardens, the Trenton police came to the club before the show anticipating trouble, given the chaotic nature of the band's performances. But when the cops walked into the dressing room they found the band calmly sitting and eating vegetarian food.(Randy Ellis, who booked City Gardens, would hire a caterer based nearby in New Jersey who could provide the Plasmatics with the type of healthy food they requested in their contract rider.)

Wendy walked up to the police officers, shook their hands and politely said, "Hello officers, how can we help you?" much to the cops' surprise.

Also, the Plasmatics performed at City Gardens three times and never requested beer or liquor in their dressing room. "They were the only band that played there who never asked for booze," Ellis said in a 2018 interview. Ellis also remarked that, as was very much the case with the Plasmatics, bands that played heavier, harder and louder music were often more pleasant and easygoing people to deal with than bands whose music was more low-key and placid.

Standing 6'7", sporting a blue Mohawk and often clad in unusual outfits, Richie Stotts's outré onstage appearance with the Plasmatics took its cue from Wendy. "When I saw Wendy take her top off I said to Rod and Wendy, 'I gotta up my game here,' and they were like, 'Go ahead,' Stotts said. "I sprayed my hair silver and then I realized that was kind of phony, then I dyed it and *that* was kinda phony. Then I was watching the movie *Taxi Driver* and I called up Rod and I said *[regarding having hair cut in a Mohawk]* "What do you think? Everyone's gonna have *[a Mohawk]* soon; everyone's going to do this –which was *not true*. My girlfriend flipped out when I got a Mohawk," said Stotts.

"I refused to wear a hat *ever* when I had a Mohawk," he continues. "I wore it through Texas, through Europe. The worst reaction I got from my Mohawk was here in the East Village. The best reaction I got was in Wyoming. Then I'm like 'Ok, the Mohawk's not good enough,' so then I dyed it blue."

When the Plasmatics performed, Richie's eyes often looked crossed – in reality, they're not. His crossing his eyes was just another aspect of how being a Plasmatic gave the band's members the license to be as out-there as they saw fit—to, paraphrasing Jimi Hendrix, let their freak flag fly.

In addition to Stotts' blue Mohawk, he started wearing costumes when the Plasmatics played: "I saw this movie with Michael Caine. He plays a male nurse dressed up like a killer and he was a maniac as a nurse and that was kind of sexual," Stotts explained when asked about his onstage attire. "Then the whole thing with the Dolls and Bowie would do drag and felt like that's a great sexual expression but it's a man doing it instead of trying to be in drag."

"Once I got on that," Stotts said, "I started with a maid outfit and then I thought 'I'll wear a tutu with a maid's outfit or a tutu with a nurse outfit,' I went to one of these stores around here *[the West Village of Manhattan]* and I got a leotard and put things in it. It was like a character I created. Rod and Wendy were super encouraging for that but the Mohawk, that's something I created," says Stotts.

That's perhaps true, as other cutting edge music performers would follow suit and wear their hair in a Mohawk. Bow Wow Wow singer Annabella Lwin sported a Mohawk in the early `80s. She blithely remarked on the New York City area music TV show *We're Dancin'* that a friend cut her hair that way while they were riding a London bus. Also in the early `80s, Joe Strummer, lead singer and guitarist for British punk band The Clash, had his hair cut in a near-to-the-scalp Mohawk that bore a very close resemblance to Robert DeNiro's hairstyle in *Taxi Driver*.

As the years went by, the Mohawk haircut would become normalized as did many other aspects of punk style. Also, as of this writing, "crazy color" hair dye in shades like pink and blue can be found at chain drugstores, Dr. Martens boots are sold at mainstream shoe stores like DSW and both these things are for sale online in the blink of a click on Amazon. In the early 2000s the "faux hawk," a men's hairdo where hair would just be combed skyward along the middle of the scalp and secured with gel or hairspray was a trend among young men, especially those categorized a "metrosexuals," meaning heterosexual men very conscious of their grooming and appearance. Circa 2007, a young woman contestant on *American Idol* wore her hair in a Mohawk while singing the Cyndi Lauper song "Time After Time." A few months after I talked with Stotts about how radical his blue Mohawk was as a Plasmatic, advertisements for UGG boots would appear in the New York City subway system featuring a young male model with his natural-looking brown hair cut in a Mohawk.

After bassist Chosei Funahara's departure, Jean Beauvoir took over on bass for the Plasmatics. Beauvoir was born in Chicago but grew up on Long Island, New York. "My uncle was a very well-known voodoo priest, Max Beauvoir. I spent summers with him," he said in a 2019 interview. "My whole other side of the family were diplomats. I was kicked out of my house when I was 14 for doing music, so I left and found myself on the streets of New York and from being in a punk band that's how I joined the Plasmatics."

Beauvoir cut a striking figure as a Plasmatic – a black man (which was a rarity in rock bands—more especially punk bands -- in the late '70s) wearing a white tuxedo with wraparound sunglasses and his hair styled in a bleach blonde Mohawk. "Anything that was out of the ordinary was something that we wanted do," he explains, "like all the crazy antics we wanted to add to the show, just being out there and doing whatever you wanted to do.

"I was actually opening for the Plasmatics in the New York Niggers, which was a punk band," Beauvoir continues when asked about how he joined Wendy, Richie and guitarist Wes Beech. "I was the lead singer. We were opening for the Plasmatics at My Father's Place on Long Island, a small club.

Video footage Of Plasmatics performing At My Father's Place in 1979 finds Wendy onstage in 1950's style women's underwear – white girdle-style panties with garters and a white bra. The band plays "Want You (Baby)" and "Sometimes I" and the way Wendy moves onstage has an almost playful aura but that doesn't last long; at one point she fires a machine gun loaded with blanks over the heads of the audience. She also smashes a large drum and prowls the stage with the drum's skin in her mouth. She leaves the stage and the club's spotlight focuses on Richie Stotts, clad in black stockings and black mini-dress and he plays an extended guitar solo with his white flying vee guitar. At this gig, the Plasmatics were using Orange brand amplifiers, renowned for their vintage sound. During this solo, Stotts lies on the stage as he plays. Wendy comes back to the stage, wearing a grey, one-piece bodice, he blonde hair is in a ponytail.

"I met their manager and everybody else and we all got along. And a little while later I saw an ad for the Plasmatics and I called them up and said, 'I hear you're looking for a bass player' so I auditioned. The auditions went on for a bit and then I got the offer. They wanted to add more musical aspects to the band and I was looking to do something crazy, I was a bit crazy myself. We were all rebels so I felt right at home. I guess the next year things really took off for us."

"Before the Plasmatics I had a stint as the lead singer of a 1950s band called The Flamingos, of all people," Beauvoir says. "They had a big hit in the '50s called "I Only Have Eyes For You." They wanted a young singer. I was wearing a tuxedo that was too big for me... I went and got my Mohawk – Richie and I had Mohawks and Wendy got hers after us. I had a white stripe in my hair and a shaved head for a while then I got it. The look just all came together: the suit, the Mohawk, cool little glasses. Bleaching my hair blonde was a lot of work and it was difficult to get it blonde without it falling out."

A landmark concert for the Plasmatics was when they performed at New York's Pier 62 on the Hudson River in the summer of 1980. Video footage of this event shows thousands of fans assembled on the Pier. Many were standing on the rooftops of nearby warehouses. The Plasmatics arrived at this gig by helicopter. Film footage of the band inside the helicopter shows Wendy pulling a white tee shirt on; she is not wearing a bra. Wendy looks out the window of the helicopter with a very focused, calm expression.

At this concert, after the Plasmatics played a short set, Wendy drove a Cadillac towards the stage and jumped out of it seconds before the car crashed into the speakers onstage, the whole stage exploded and the Cadillac plunged into the Hudson River.

"It was an interesting time," says Jean Beauvoir. "Everyone in New York showed up, people on rooftops, every news channel. We became an *Eyewitness News* commercial for a while. We had to deal with the cops and the Fire Department but they were all very cool and supportive of the band and the craziness we were doing. We were hassled to an extent but more by fire marshals because of the explosives we used. They'd always come to us before the show."

At Pier 62, an officer from the NYPD addressed the crowd in a very calm manner, matter-of-factly saying, "The band will perform, then an automobile will crash into the speakers and then go into the Hudson. Then the show will be over, so please disperse in an orderly fashion so we can all enjoy the show and everyone will get home safe."

The stage was decorated with vases of flowers and a giant white sarcophagus/coffin-like structure decorated with red Asian alphabet characters (The Plasmatics often counted off songs by saying "ichi ni san shi" which is 1-2-3-4 in Japanese). At this concert Wendy is wearing pale pink knee-length tight pants, the aforementioned white tee, white sneakers and a pink motorcycle jacket. There are splashes of pink in Wendy's blonde hair, which is pulled back into a ponytail. The other members of the Plasmatics are playing for a substantial amount of time before Wendy comes onstage, takes the mic and warmly greets the crowd by saying "Hello New York, we're the Plasmatics!" The band then plays "Squirm."

"We rehearsed a lot. We did a lot of pre-concert preparation, they built the stage," says Stu Deutsch, Plasmatics drummer at that time, when asked about the Pier 62 show. "It was a dangerous thing to do, because there were gas tanks underneath the stage for the explosions. I think we only did five songs. There were so many people there; 15,000, 20,000, I don't know. They just kept showing up. We had to go there by helicopter because we couldn't get there otherwise."

According to Stu Deutsch, there was a big gap between the stage and the audience for the crowd's protection and a very strong police and fire department presence.

"So we get off the helicopter, we get on the stage," Deutsch explains, "we do the songs and they rigged the car –it had no brakes – it was rigged so that when Wendy hit the accelerator it would keep going. So the middle of the last song, it think it was "Nothing," a Jean Beauvoir song, Wendy put on a helmet, she's got her pink leather jacket on and she gets into the car – it had no door so she could get out – and she aimed it at the stage. When we saw she was there at the stage we got off the stage; we ran. And it hit and you see the car go into the stage and the whole thing exploding."

"I was scared to death," Wendy said to Richard Harrington in the November 22, 1980 issue of *The Washington Post*, discussing the stunt at Pier 62, "but I love the combination of fear and excitement. Sitting through a Plasmatics show and coming out alive gives everybody a group feeling, an instant orgasmic rush. It's 1980s rock 'n roll, which is what everybody's looking for."

The Pier 62 show was "pivotal," Jean Beauvoir says, "because nobody knew what we were going to do and we always did something unorthodox. And that show started the Pier concerts because there were never concerts there before."

(As the Eighties progressed, The Pier, as it came to be known, staged summer evening concerts by notable Alternative acts such as The Cure, The Psychedelic Furs, U2, The Smiths and Echo and The Bunnymen.)

"We had to retrieve the car from the Hudson River," Deutsch recalls," we couldn't just leave it there. We hired a company to do that. There was an ambulance that took Wendy and us out of the place and Wendy was fine."

Video footage of the Pier 62 concert shows Wendy in an ambulance after she had jumped out of the car before the stage exploded. She insists "I'm fine! I'm fine!" When she's asked how she feels she tears off her oxygen mask and exclaims, "I feel fuckin' great!"

Wendy told Carol Wallace, reporter for *People* Magazine in 1983, "It's not that I don't value my life, it's just that I love taking chances, testing myself, stepping over the line. It's fun. It's a turn on."

"I always knew I had a message, but I didn't know what it was," Wendy said to Wallace. The message Wendy was sending on Pier 62 that day was solidifying her standing as rock music's supreme daredevil—male or female.

In her interview in the November 22, 1980 issue of *The Washington Post,* Wendy talks about the vision she had of an ultimate Plasmatics concert, possibly in the Nevada desert and running over a couple of days. Like the Pier 62 concert admission would be free. "We'll build a city in the middle of nowhere, with the only way of getting to it and the show being by mule train. Food and water will be brought in the same way and rationed out."

Describing this event further, Wendy says: "As we're singing and playing, the city will be leveled to the ground. When we've run out of songs and we've maybe blown up a blimp overhead with an airplane of helicopter, everyone will have to leave by mule train. This is what gets us off."

Wendy made this statement six years before the first Burning Man – the quasi tribal temporary city in the desert built to be destroyed that would become an annual event to this day. One could maybe see some similarity between the two concepts, but as Burning Man grew in popularity—and regularly took place in the Nevada desert— several LLC companies were formed to administer to it. One can imagine Wendy not wanting such a structure for the event she described.

The Plasmatics reportedly bought the 1972 Cadillac for their Pier 62 show secondhand from a couple who were wary of selling it to the band just to be demolished and sink into the Hudson River. Wendy said to them, "Your car isn't going to be destroyed – it's going to become immortal." When I interviewed Beauvoir for this book, I remarked to him that Wendy said this and he replied, "That's totally Wendy."

Even though thousands of fans flocked to Pier 62 to see the Plasmatics that day, the band had their detractors, such as rock journalist/performer Mick Farren, who pointed out in the December 1980 issue of *Trouser Press* that smashing TV sets and destroying a car as part of a rock band's act was not something new under the sun. "In 1967, The Move smashed TV sets and a Chevy onstage to promote their single 'Night of Fear,'" he wrote.

When Farren, MC5 co-founder Wayne Kramer and Kramer's girlfriend Sam showed up too late to Pier 62 to see Wendy jump out of the Cadillac that crashed into the wall of exploding speakers and plunged into the Hudson, he reported that audience members weren't particularly excited by what had taken place. In that same previously mentioned issue of *Trouser Press,* Farren writes about poking his head out of Kramer's (ironically) brand new Cadillac and talking to someone who had just seen the show. Farren's exchange with the concertgoer went thusly:

"How was it?"

"Passerby shrugs. 'It was okay.' Passerby has second thoughts. 'It was good. Yeah it was good.'"

"Did she dive out of the car at the last minute?"

"Yeah."

"And the stage blew up?"

"Yeah. It was okay."

Chalk that up maybe to New Yorkers' perennial seen-it-all demeanor or a sense of wonder numbed by too many cars going kaboom on TV -- Farren points out that in 1980 cars blew up on the CBS-TV show *The Dukes of Hazard* every week.

But there *were* thousands of people in the audience at the Pier 62 show cheering Wendy on as she did her stunt. There *was* palpable excitement in that crowd. Maybe Farren just got there too late and missed out. As the saying goes, "you had to be there."

Farren went on to write that "...the kind of non-music, rock 'n' roll geek show that is the Plasmatics' stock in trade has become routine, something of little note beyond a couple of hours' diversion and the cheapest of cheap thrills."

Wendy, though, saw cathartic value in the Plasmatics' explosive performances:

"People come to see us, the sweat starts flowing, the blood starts moving, they get their release and everybody goes home and nobody gets hurt," she once said.

"It was like being an actress for her," Ida Langsam says. "It was like playing a part. She was a show woman."

Something significant about the Plasmatics is their lack of nihilism contrasting with their appetite for destruction. The Merriam-Webster dictionary says nihilism is "a doctrine or belief that conditions in the social organization are so bad as to make destruction desirable for its own sake independent of any constructive program or possibility."

In Griel Marcus's book *Lipstick Traces – A Secret History of the 20th Century* , he writes: "[Vasily] Rozanov's definition of nihilism is the best, 'situationist Raoul Vaneigem had said in 1967 in *Traite de savoire faire a l' usage de jeunes generations* (*Treatise For The Young Generations*, known in the U.S. as *The Revolution of Everyday Life*). The show is over, the audience gets up to leave their seats. Time to collect their coats and go home. They turn round…No more coats and no more home.'"

The Plasmatics weren't nihilists. There is a certain unusual optimism in the Plasmatics destroying big-ticket objects and combatting materialism. There was something aspirational in their destroying cars, TV sets etc. during their concerts. If they were truly nihilists they would have been *self*-destructive for self-destruction's sake. They would have had substance abuse problems like punk nihilism icon Sid Vicious or Kurt Cobain--in contrast, Wendy was virulently opposed to drugs and alcohol. By destroying objects and making a statement about anti-materialism, their stance encouraged their audience to think and not just be passively entertained. They were saying, don't put all your energy into buying a bigger car and don't covet a bigger television. Stop worshiping big-ticket objects and focus your energy elsewhere.

"The Plasmatics were sort of what square middle America's idea of what a punk band was, just completely over the top and purposely cartoonish," opines Paul Bruno, creator and curator of The Unblinking Ear podcast, label head at Unblinking Ear Records and frequent DJ on radio station WFMU. "They could have replaced the strawman bands in *CHiPS* or *Quincy MD's* punk episodes and no one would have batted an eye. Their act may seem silly now (and was likely silly to "serious" punks then) but they were calculated to give young fans transgressive thrills and make parents recoil in horror at the debauchery. Which isn't to say they didn't make some decent records," he concludes, adding, "Sincerity is hardly a prerequisite in popular music."

"I went to Plasmatics gigs and wrote them up for publications like *US* magazine, where I was the music columnist, and the *SoHo Weekly*

News," says Michael Musto, noted nightlife/culture journalist for the *Village Voice*, *The Advocate* and other publications. "I also did a feature on them for *Interview* Magazine, where they glammed them up for a photo shoot. I was thrilled to get the Plasmatics into *Interview*. I didn't think they were great art but I loved the brio, energy, humor and Wendy's punk goddess persona. We were all friends, and I'm still friends with Chosei, but I once wrote something Wendy didn't like and she left me a blistering message on my answering machine. It was a real takedown – fuming and very confrontational – and I realized the punk thing wasn't an act."

When asked to elaborate, Musto says: "I had written a negative write-up about their music at that point, and I used a quote she had previously given me and she said, 'If you're going to trash me, you could have called me for new quotes!'"

The Man Who Changed Wendy's Life

Once Wendy met Rod Swenson circa 1976 and found work at Captain Kink's Sex Fantasy Theater, she found her niche and a sense of home with Rod that she didn't have before. "She just came alive in that environment," Swenson told the *Rochester Democrat and Chronicle* in 2016, "in a way she found some place she had been looking for since she left home," Swenson says. "It was amazing, how fast she came alive."

Having earned an MFA from Yale, Swenson brought an artistic sensibility to Captain Kink's Sex Fantasy Theater. Situated in New York's Times Square, this set it apart from the fairly sleazy types of entertainment on offer in that part of Manhattan during those days. There was nothing like his theater in Times Square at that time (nor has there been anything like it since, given the current family-focused tourist trap atmosphere of the area).

Swenson approached Times Square theaters that were faring poorly – old vaudeville/strip joints with hardly any patrons coming to see junkie strippers in timeworn spangly outfits. There'd be maybe two or three raincoat-clad men in the audience; some nodding out, and some, well, doing things under their raincoats that men do while watching such women on stage. Business at these theaters was slow, so Swenson made an arrangement with the owner of one such theater on 42nd Street.

He put on a show of 20-minute vignettes that lasted an hour and dealt with a variety of subjects: some political, some radical, a lot having sexual orientation. Swenson promoted these shows via advertising and word-of-mouth. Soon, Captain Kink's Sex Fantasy Theater started drawing a following beyond the men in raincoats.

Then different theaters asked Swenson to stage performances of what was shaping up to be a repertory company. Players in this group would come and go. When Swenson placed the casting call ad in *Show Business* he met Wendy.

In 1977, Swenson's creative impulses were thriving in his Times Square theater operation as he staged a growing number of performances. He viewed the late 1970s, pre-1990s sanitization/Disneyfication of that area of Manhattan as an anything-goes hotbed of experimentation where there were no rules as long as big enough audiences were drawn to cover the overhead. "It was a lab of sorts," Swenson told *Noisey*, "and each week we launched a new show on Monday. It seated about 150 people and we ended up running five shows a day beginning at lunchtime seven days a week.

The new show for each week had to be written by and then blocked and run-through Sunday night after the theatre closed at midnight to be ready to open for the early matinee on Monday so Sunday nights the whole time I did shows there we never slept. We never sold advance tickets and there was always a line for our opening show on Monday and many of our shows typically sold out."

"There was nothing sleazy about them at all," Wendy said to Phil Sutcliffe in the May 31, 1980 issue of *Sounds,* regarding the performances at Captain Kink's Sex Fantasy Theater. "It wasn't just a girl walking on stage and fucking. This was not a sex show. Some numbers were funny, some of them were terrifying, and some of them were just sexy. There was a Victorian one, a Western show, animals; girls were dressed like gorillas or horses or dogs."

"I liked it being slightly illegal," Wendy continues. "I was arrested over a hundred times - I loved it. They'd take me down to the precinct and keep me there for a while and see if they could make me miss a coupla shows."

There's some back-and-forth in Sutcliffe's interview as to how explicit the shows were. Swenson is quoted as saying, "I don't know why she's saying there weren't guys and girls fucking on stage because there were." Wendy then replies, "In the last couple maybe. It wasn't the main constituent of the show there."

Swenson then says, "Her specialty was the girl-to-girl numbers. She did perform hardcore sex but not with men onstage. It was a hard as you can get --oral sex, penetration with…whatever."

"I'm not a lesbian," Wendy retorts, "I'm bisexual. I like girls as much as guys." Years later in 1984, on an episode of the *Sally Jessy Rafael* television talk show, Wendy casually remarks, "I like guys, I like girls, whatever. I just like people who treat other people like human beings."

Exciting things were also happening further downtown at CBGB and Max's Kansas City – a scene Swenson also viewed as a bubbling test kitchen of creativity and inspiration. Circa 1977, Swenson was intrigued by the punk music scene happening in downtown New York and saw it as a vibrant place not just for music but for art, performance-- anything. (Swenson saw live music as an element that was missing in his Times Square theatrical productions). He filmed videos for The Ramones, Blondeie and The Dead Boys. "I think I was the first to put on a show with Patti Smith in an actual theater-sized venue in New York larger than CBGB's -- the then-Elgin Theatre in Chelsea, which I also took over briefly," he told *Noisey*.

Wendy arrived in New York via bus at this time with very little money and no real connections. She saw the ad for "experimental performers" at Captain Kink's Sex Fantasy Theater that Swenson placed in *Show Business* on the floor of the Port Authority Bus Terminal. As Swenson told *Killdren* magazine in 2008: "She applied for a job, and as she would tell me later, from the minute we met she knew she had found what she was looking for. 'It was like I'd arrived on a different planet,' she'd say."

"You see I was an utter counter-culture radicalist too," Swenson explains in the *Killdren* interview, "bent on finding authenticity, challenging the status quo, and rejecting the mores of the world in almost the identical way she did. She'd never encountered anything like that and neither had I."

In late 1977, Swenson was so inspired by Wendy and the bands he was seeing, that he decided to form a rock band with Wendy as the star. "I was working with Wendy on the the Plasmatics and pretty soon, as that took off, and for the better part of the next ten years, that took almost all my time and attention," he told *Noisey*.

In addition to managing the Plasmatics, Swenson did creative work for the band, using tongue-in-cheek pseudonyms. He photographed their album covers, did album art and shot promotional stills using the name "Butch Star," ("We would often get calls at the office from record labels or others who wanted to know how to get a hold of Butch Star to hire to do a shoot or do some art work for them," Swenson told *Noisey*.) He wrote lyrics for Plasmatics songs using the name "Stellar Axeman." On Plasmatics albums he would be credited as "Concept and Management: Rod Swenson."

"Among the reasons that I started doing it was simply so that the well-deserved attention would go to Wendy," Swenson told *Noisey*.

"Yes, I did all these things, but she was the star, it was built with and around her. It was also kind of part of the inside stuff that people who really knew something about the band knew but the average off-the-street person didn't."

In the *Noisey* interview, Swenson is asked about "some journalists" saying that he was a Svengali to Wendy. In response he cites Wendy's courage to break stereotypes and because of this, establishment types found her threatening. "As any number of actual journalists have pointed out," Swenson said, "Wendy, with the great courage she had, broke all kinds of stereotypes and so various establishment types found her threatening. I would say a remark like that, implicitly kind of old-school sexist, would be from someone in that category."

Swenson and Wendy were romantically involved and in a monogamous relationship, which seems to stand in contrast to Wendy's sexually provocative onstage manner. "Wendy in real life was nothing like her stage persona," says Greg Smith, bassist in Wendy's post-Plasmatics solo band. W.O.W. "She was a very sweet person. There of course were Wendy groupies but she was dedicated to her relationship with Rod."

The idea of Wendy being very sexual in performance yet not being promiscuous in her personal life is a sort of testament to her subversion and adds a layer of meaning to her character. It would be very easy to jump to the conclusion that a woman performing onstage virtually topless, simulating masturbation and slicing apart guitars in a quasi-erotic manner would be oversexed offstage. Instead it's as if she was challenging her audience's definition of female sexuality in the arena of rock music while onstage, yet she kept her actual sexuality private and personal; very much taking ownership of it in a healthy and sustaining manner.

Having a large amount of random sexual partners in the late Seventies and early to mid-Eighties – the years in which the Plasmatics were their most famous – was, in retrospect, not a good idea as the AIDS crisis was emerging then. By just being with Rod Swenson, Wendy was protecting herself, in a sense, whether she was aware of this or not.

Both Wendy and Swenson resisted being categorized, positioning themselves in opposition to any sort of -ism or -ist suffix that would define them as a type or kind. Specifically regarding whether Wendy thought of herself as a feminist, Wendy and Swenson decried the commodification of feminism into solely a white, middle-class "career woman" mindset and stressed that Wendy stood up for women in a field that was male-biased, chauvinistic, misogynistic and male-oriented -- her stance was as an uncompromising woman in a very much male-dominated rock scene.

"She opened the door – without intending to – for a whole generation of not just musicians or rockers but for women's lib." says Ida Langsam.

Jack Mulholland recalled an encounter that was somewhat revelatory to the nature of Wendy and Rod's relationship: "I was a member of the Plasmatics' fan club, the Secret Service. I used the Secret Service card to get into Plasmatics shows for free. So I was good all over town, so I used the Secret Service card to get into the Plasmatics show in Champaign-Urbana Illinois. Now I was in Champaign-Urbana because I had a girlfriend there. This is significant. Her name was Shonnie, God bless her soul she died, she was only 59 when she died. She was a very beautiful blondee, she had huge brown doe eyes.

"I used my Secret Service card to get in the show for free and then after the show, the dressing rooms were upstairs, Wendy had her own dressing room and Shonnie and I went upstairs and we saw Wendy in this dressing room and we went into the room and started making small talk. Wendy was very friendly, so we're complimenting her on the show, her theatrics, her moves – just the way she projected herself on stage. So it was a very fun conversation. The door to the dressing room was open. After about 15 minutes of conversation with Wendy, making small talk, Rod Swenson walked by and he stopped and he looked in and he gave Shonnie and I a very hard stare. He didn't say anything but the impression Shonnie and I got was that he really did not welcome us being alone with Wendy. Call it intuition if you will, but we felt it so we politely dismissed ourselves.

"Wendy didn't ask us to leave," recalls Mulholland. "I found it odd because I never knew for certain if Rod had a romantic relationship with Wendy but because of this incident in Champaign-Urbana I felt that he was very possessive of her.

"The reason I bring up the fact that I was with my girlfriend is that Rod would have had no reason if he was in love with Wendy and they had a romantic relationship and he was jealous of any other man being around her, he had no reason to be jealous under these circumstances because I was there with a beautiful woman of my own – and we were just making small talk. That's when I got this feeling…this sensation of hostility from Rod, that we were not welcome there.

"After that the rest of the Plasmatics, except Wendy, all went to a party at the promoter's house, and that's a whole other story, what went on there," says Mulholland. "Not only the band members but the pyrotechnics guy Peter Capadoccia – who I just knew as Peter Extra-- who was trying to put the make on Shonnie and get her to get in the Ryder truck to go to the next gig. I couldn't blame him. She was a very beautiful woman."

Wendy had ardent female fans. In an article in *The Boston Globe* written by Jim Sullivan in 1981, Wendy said "I think girls like coming to Plasmatics shows and having me up front doing my stuff and having someone to relate to."

Bunny Hirsch, singer and bassist for the New York City-based band Perp Walk is a fan of Wendy's. "She was totally original," Hirsch says, "She did her own thing! She had her own mind." When asked if she's inspired by Wendy, Hirsch answers "YES!" adding, "I played the clarinet in school, too. I wish I could wear a bikini on stage and look as good as her. She was a great role model who does NOT conform. She just wore and said whatever the hell she wanted. Such stage presence! And her healthy lifestyle on the road (diet, exercise, not drinking) should be emulated too."

The Los Angeles-based metal band Butcher Babies – fronted by Carla Harvey and Heidi Shepherd, named themselves after the Plasmatics' most famous song and cite Wendy as a main influence. Shepherd and Harvey both grew up under difficult circumstances: Shepherd was raised Mormon in a repressive Utah environment and was abused as a child. Harvey is biracial, endured substantial prejudice in a racially divided town, and her father abandoned her family. In an article written by Michael Freidman, PhD., in the May 11, 2018 edition of *Psychology Today.com*, Heidi Shepherd and Carla Harvey discussed how they found Wendy inspirational. Shepherd had been enthralled by Williams, by seeing her perform for the first time, and she referred to Wendy as the "first female of heavy metal; the woman who went out there and really paved the way for artists like ourselves and any other females in this industry really to take a stand and make some noise," she enthused.

The article states that Harvey and Shepherd both encountered sexism while working in different capacities for *Playboy*: Harvey was a reporter and she had to sign a contract stipulating that she had to have blonde hair and had to maintain a certain weight. Shepherd worked for *Playboy* radio and was asked to participate in a "Topless Tuesday" radio show, to which she objected.

Eventually Shepherd and Harvey found each other, bonded over their admiration for Wendy and formed Butcher Babies. At one point in their band's early days they paid homage to Wendy by wearing black electrical tape on their nipples. As Shepherd said of Wendy: "...she was wearing that against the repression of women . . . where they tell you what you're supposed to look like, what you're supposed to sound like. They try to dictate everything about you. And she went out there and was like 'F*ck that sh*t. I'm going to be who I want to be and sound like I want to sound — just to spite you.' And it was a message and a movement."

"We started this band, it was basically an ode to Wendy O. Williams," Shepherd continues, "What I really love about the movement that Wendy started was that it was OK to be yourself. If you feel a certain way about yourself, write about it, sing it, be it. Her outfit choice was what our outfit choice was," Shepherd said. "For us, we really stood by what Wendy started. It was like, 'F*ck that, I'm going to look like I want to look, dress how I want to dress, be how I want to be, make the music how I want to make it, sound how I want to sound.'"

The statement both Wendy and the women in Butcher Babies made by performing with their breasts bare except for black tape over their nipples was one of choice and self-determination. *They* decided to appear that way.

"Fast forward when me and Heidi started Butcher Babies and wore the nipple tape, it was a different feeling," said Harvey in the *Psychology Today.com* article. "It wasn't like I was a packaged blondee *Playboy* girl with no brain. I was using the tools I wanted to use my whole life," Harvey said. "We were writing music. We were getting out all of the anger we had, all the emotions we felt, and it was a very cathartic experience. Even going up there with nipple tape on, it was very cathartic for us to perform and be ourselves for the first time in a lot of ways. It was a liberation from being what everyone else wanted us to be for years."

Fernando Bonenfant from the *Metal Wani* website conducted an interview with Harvey and Shepherd where Harvey echoes the kind of focused self-possession that Wendy had, updated for the Internet age. Harvey told Bonenfant: "If you let what people say online bother you every day of your life, you'll lead a miserable existence. My personal life is clear of all the Internet drama. Who cares? And, obviously, it's been nine years since we started the band. We're a lot different now than we were nine years ago. But we've had to just let it go and not care."

The Brainwashed Do Not Know They Are Brainwashed

When a band without a recording contract regularly sells out venues, generates a big fan following on their own, and receives a large amount of glowing press, record companies typically line up with pens and contracts in hand hoping to cash in and have such a band make records for them. But circa 1979, when the Plasmatics were destroying TVs and blowing up cars on stage in front of enthusiastic, adoring audiences, most record labels were perplexed – and frankly a bit frightened--as to how they could turn such a band into hit making recording artists.

They kept their distance from the Plasmatics, despite the notoriety and rather professional self-containment of the band. On one hand, the Plasmatics would have benefitted from the financial and administrative support of a record company but on the other hand they were able to build up a fan base and perform the kind of concerts they wanted to without them so far.

Regarding record companies, Rod Swenson told Chris Knowles from *Classic Rock.com*: "They were signing these bands, and the only way they could go out on the road was with 50 grand of tour support. We were able to pay for ourselves and blow up automobiles."

The Plasmatics did release "Butcher Baby" as a single and an EP titled *Meet the Plasmatics* on their own Vice Squad label, but in 1979 or so a self- released record could only get so much attention.

The irreverent independent British recording company Stiff Records saw potential in the Plasmatics and signed them to their United States division, Stiff America.

Stiff was known for their cheeky advertising -- their famous slogan was "If it Ain't Stiff It Ain't Worth A Fuck." Stiff's artist roster included Nick Lowe, The Damned, Ian Dury and the Blockheads and Lene Lovich, among other artists. When asked in a 2019 interview why he wanted to sign the Plasmatics, Stiff co-founder David Robinson said: "They were really over the top in their live show standards and I thought they had the essence of punk musically." Did Robinson think that the iconoclastic company culture of Stiff seemed like a good place for such a band of renegades? "Yes that had an effect," he says, "but I think that also nobody else would touch them at that time and they needed a record company." About Wendy, Robinson says, "She didn't seem to have any boundaries of what she wouldn't do."

The Plasmatics' debut LP, *New Hope For The Wretched* was released in the US on Stiff America on October 2, 1980.

There are twelve songs on *New Hope For The Wretched* and most of them are rather short. The album begins with "Tight Black Pants" a burst of lusty energy as Wendy growls "let's go somewhere/wanna make it with you." Her vocals are truly unique for a woman singer emerging circa 1980; Wendy's voice is rough and aggressive as Wes and Richie's guitars burst forth with searing short sharp shocks.

During that time, some of the most popular women singers -- Olivia Newton-John and Pat Benatar, for example—topped the charts by sounding conventional. Unlike them, Wendy's voice is abrasive and confrontational.

"Monkey Suit" has a meat hook catchiness and is a rather danceable tirade against people who would come to be known as yuppies ("monkey suit" being a slang term for stifling suit-and-tie corporate workwear). Accompanied by significant cowbell on "Monkey Suit," Wendy brays, "There you go/but you ain't going nowhere/you got money/ but it ain't buying you nothing," The songs on *New Hope For The Wretched*, written by Swenson in collaboration with Stotts, rhythm guitarist Wes Beech and Funahara, cast a critical eye on a toxic society (hence the album's title). Also, years before the term "couch potato" came into parlance, TV addicts and video vegetables are the target of Wendy's ire on "Living Dead": "You've got ideas/in your head/ They won't happen/ you're the living dead."

"Test Tube Babies" could very well be construed as a love song – Wendy punctuatingly pants "I love you," though it's not exactly clear to whom she's directing her affection. "Concrete Shoes" tells of a phone being tapped and hints at organized crime goings-on. A video for this song has footage of men wearing hoods driving to a waterfront and throwing what may be a body into what might be the Hudson River (no doubt wearing the end-of-the-line footwear of the song's title).

"Squirm," is a recording of the Plasmatics performing live with enthusiastic crowd noise at the end. The countoff of "ichi, ni,san,shi" introduces "Want You Baby" a song that has been in the Plasmatics repertoire since their early days.Here Wendy's vocals are a tirade of the libido – she wants who she wants and sounds like nothing will stop her. In a similar vein is the Plasmatics' version of the 1960s Bobby Darin hit "Dream Lover." Instead of sounding like a hopeful, wishful ingénue, Wendy's vocals are demanding, insistent. In the song's very long bridge, the guitars and drums sound like they're collapsing, falling over each other. The song's key guitar riff signals the return of Wendy's vocals.

"Sometimes I" is a song where Wendy sings the title phrase over and over, making it sound like a raw yet contemplative mantra. "Sometimes I/sometimes I / feel it/when you're/when you're/down on your knees," Wendy sings with an insisting tone that's dominant with more than a hint of coaxing. "Corruption" is a whirling punk maelstrom with a bridge that sounds like rapid fire gunshots.

The album ends with "Butcher Baby, "which would become the band's signature song. The refrain of "Butcher Baby" is "oh yeah/oh no" -- expressing feelings of both pleasure and dread, sentiments that suit the Plasmatics' oeuvre perfectly: they were a band that many people were shocked by and perhaps maybe afraid of and they were also a band that had devoted fans.

"Tight Black Pants", New Hope For The Wretched's opening track, is only one minute and 44 seconds long. To begin an album with an exceptionally brief song seems like a risky move if the band wanted radio airplay. For ages, radio favored songs clocking in at around three minutes and thirty seconds or so – to have the first song on their debut album be under a minute and 45 seconds, seemed like the Plasmatics were saying they didn't care about radio.

In the years that would follow, legions of hardcore punk bands would make very brief songs their stock in trade. These bands focused heavily on live performances and touring, with hardly any concern about being played on commercial rock radio. With Wendy's growling vocals sounding nothing like the handful of women heard on typical rock stations at the time and the furious blend of punk behind her, the Plasmatics didn't compromise to court radio at all on their debut album.

Having a very brief song opening *New Hope*…may also have been an effective technique to draw the listener in to listen to the songs that follow; if a song is over just as a listener's interest is sparked, they may very well want to hear more.

Most of the songs on *New Hope For The Wretched* are less than three minutes and thirty seconds long. The longest songs on this album are their radical reworking of "Dream Lover"(5:35) and "Sometimes I" (3:51). The album *ends* with "Butcher Baby" – the Plasmatics' anthem. Placing this song at the end of the record is a clever move; a sort of challenge to the listener to hear the entire album – songs they might not be familiar with – before the payoff of hearing a song they know.

The cover of *New Hope For The Wretched* is visually arresting. The cover image consists of Wendy sitting on the roof of a white Cadillac sinking into the swimming pool at Sunshine Park – the New Jersey nudist camp Rod Swenson had been involved with. There are splashes of bright pink in Wendy's platinum blonde hair, her right breast is exposed with black tape covering her nipple. She is wearing a black lace bodice, patterned black hosiery, tall red boots and her pink motorcycle jacket. Wendy's expression is one of defiance. It's as if she is saying "Yeah, we're rendering this Cadillac useless – *so what?*"

The other members of the Plasmatics are on the cover as well. Richie is in the pool lying back in an inner tube atop the sinking hood of the Cadillac, wearing a white tutu and blue tights, his Flying Vee guitar in tow. Wes is sitting on the edge of the pool wearing his trademark football player's black on his face with his lower legs in the water as he holds an electric guitar. The cord of what appears to be an amplifier is plugged into this guitar (quite a risky move). Jean Beauvoir is reclining in a lounge chair and Stu Deutsch is about to strike a TV set with a sledgehammer.

This image of the Plasmatics on the cover of *New Hope For The Wretched* further emphasizes the stance the band took against materialism. The objects in the cover photo are the same things they would destroy on stage – a Cadillac, a TV, an electric guitar. Yet here these big-ticket items are being rendered useless in and around a swimming pool - a quintessential luxury purchase for suburban families. This tableau makes a visual threat against the middle class that Wendy refused to be a part of.

The actual record of *New Hope For The Wretched*, when it was first issued by Stiff, was far from your typical black vinyl long player. Early editions of the album contained a vinyl disc in marbleized green, yellow and orange. The label featured a red cross/plus sign on a white background – this red symbol would soon appear on Plasmatics' amplifiers. Later editions of the album have a disc in marbleized pink and white, solid orange and a shade of pink similar to the one Wendy would wear in her platinum blonde hair.

Inside the jacket of New Hope For The Wretched was a flyer advertising the Plasmatics' fan club—the Secret Service. The copy on it has a very take-no-prisoners tone, saying in boldface type:

Are you a woman or a wimp? Are you a man or a mouse? Are you a paranoid vegetable or do you have the guts to take aggressive action? Join the Plasmatics Secret Service.

FIGHT AUTHORITY! Are you sick of people telling you what to do? Do boring radio stations and mealy-mouthed DJs make you barf? Do phony incompetent rock critics who like to play it safe make you want to go out and do something violent? Take a stand! Fill out the coupon below and mail in your $10 (ten bucks) today or have you been intimidated into SUBMISSION?

DON'T BE STUPID. Don't be the one to miss out. Look here's what you get:

1) **Exclusive red & silver enamel Plasmatic pin-only available to secret service members. Tells those who know exactly where you stand.**
2) **Exclusive giant poster not for sale to the general public. A real collector's item.**
3) **A personally signed photo.**
4) **Official Plasmatic Secret Service membership card good for merchandise discounts and special offers.**
5) **Official Secret Service quarterly newsletter including advance information on concerts, recordings, merchandise etc.**

Send to Plasmatics Secret Service c/o Stiff Records 157 W, 57th Street New York, NY 10019

Ten dollars in 1980 could have bought you two movie tickets for an evening's entertainment, according to Slate.com. But given that there were five items offered in the Plasmatic Secret Service membership at the value of maybe more than two dollars each and they weren't available anywhere else, that was a pretty good deal. Especially if you were a big fan.

Rolling Stone, well established as the bible of rock journalism at the time of *New Hope For The Wretched*'s release, was not kind to this debut album by the Plasmatics. Writer David Fricke called the Plasmatics "motley New York jokers," and wrote "The Plasmatics should be seen and not heard" in his one-star review of *New Hope For The Wretched*.

Tim Sommer is a noted music journalist who has been a VH1 and MTV television personality, an A&R executive at Atlantic Records and host of Noise the Show—New York University radio station WNYU's influential early Eighties punk and hardcore program. In a 2019 interview for this book he posits that, in the late '70s to the early '80s, American mainstream culture – mass media and the major record label-controlled music industry, were "very much aligned against the dissemination and acceptance of new music/punk rock in the United States, this is very much the opposite of the situation in Great Britain, where, I think, the media and the mainstream music industry very much saw that punk rock could help their interests, and boost their bottom line -- but the *[U.S.]* mainstream media (i.e. *Rolling Stone*) and virtually all of the major record labels virtually conspired to shut down anything that threatened the comfortable old guard.

"This encouraged outsized characters," Sommer continues "like, say, Williams or*[Dead Kennedys singer and political gadfly]*Jello Biafra -- who wanted to use whatever was at their disposal to create a profile that somehow CUT THROUGH the walls traditional media had constructed. To put it a different way, Tom Verlaine couldn't make a dent on the charts or Rolling Stone, so to make America pay attention to the fact that the old guard was falling, outsized characters needed to do something that might grab time on the evening news (Williams chainsawing cars, Biafra running for office)."

As Sommer explains, "What was extraordinary about the Plasmatics wasn't their music, but their desire to cut through the forces that had conspired to SHUT DOWN and block the natural evolution of culture and music via whatever tools were necessary.... The U.K. for instance, WELCOMED a Johnny Rotten because the labels and the newspapers and the TV shows knew he was good for business -- but in America, the old guard wanted to keep that door FIRMLY SHUT, which meant that the outrage had to be THAT much more extreme..."1994.

People magazine, in its January 26, 1981 Picks and Pans reviews section, *did* give *New Hope For The Wretched* a qualified thumbs up. Crediting the review to "*People* Staff" the magazine said:

"Transcending the normal bounds of wretchedness, the Plasmatics reach a new plateau of raging infantilism and epic depravity. In other words they're so excessively bad they're sort of terrific...Modeled after the Ramones, the Plasmatics make music that is crude, loud, urgent and perversely danceable. They're the amphetamine hit the fading punk movement needs."

"Jimmy Miller produced our first album," says Richie Stotts, reflecting on the recording of *New Hope For The Wretched*. "Jimmy Miller is in my opinion one of the greatest producers in rock. He produced the four seminal albums by the Rolling Stones which are just the greatest: *Let it Bleed, Sticky Fingers, Exile on Main Street* and *Beggars Banquet*. Jimmy Miller had his problems, he had a loose style to him but he produced *New Hope For the Wretched*."

In the *Wendy O. Williams and the Plasmatics: 10 Years of Revolutionary Rock 'n' Roll* documentary it is stated that Jimmy Miller's heroin use interfered with his production of *New Hope For The Wretched* and production was completed by Ed Stasium. As Wes Beech states in the documentary, Jimmy Miller "...would have these disappearances where he would say: 'Excuse me for a minute' and he'd be gone for half an hour. We'd be like: 'Where'd Jimmy go?' And we'd check all the bathrooms. Once we found him passed out in the ladies' room." In a 2019 interview, Ed Stasium said *New Hope*...was completely recorded by the time he was brought in to mix it. "I just did what I always did," Stasium said, "I just turned everything all the way up."

"He pulled something out of the band for that album," Stotts continues, speaking of Jimmy Miller. "He's a great producer. I was there. the Plasmatics, the members we had in the band – we were all really good players but the natural evolution going back to Jimmy Miller, I heard the Motörhead album *Overkill [which Miller co-produced]* and I said 'this is exactly what I want to play like. This is where I'm coming from.'"(Miller died in 1994).

"Whether you liked it or not," reflects Richie Stotts on the Plasmatics' sound, "it wasn't lightweight and there was something beyond that, there was something in the music, there was an intersection of punk and metal. Before the band started I was kind of going that way. I liked the Ramones and I liked Jimi Hendrix too. Iggy and The Stooges had kind of a metal-ish punk thing going on. I think the Plasmatics were our own entity because we were beyond just a musical band.

"That's another dimension too," he explains further "because we had the punk and the metal and also the theatrical side and what was the band about? I'm not really sure. Especially in the beginning. the Plasmatics...we were indefinable. Maybe for me we were pushing the envelope in a good way, in a funny but heavy kind of way. It was right there, it was hard to deny. Some people would react poorly to it but other people would get it."

Speaking with Jason Webber from *Noisey*, in 2012, Rod Swenson discussed this factor of perception regarding the Plasmatics: "One of the things about us humans is our ability to not see what is right in front of us," he said, adding "We literally bracket things out. One of the phrases we memorialized on one of our tour T-Shirts was from a message that was edited in backwards at the end of one of our albums so you had to, in the days of turntables, spin the album backwards manually to understand it. It said "The brainwashed do not know they are brainwashed."

In the Oughts, Pear Jam lead singer Eddie Vedder was photographed wearing the Plasmatics t-shirt bearing the phrase "The Brainwashed Do Not Know They Are Brainwashed" and an image of Wendy from the era of their *Coup d' Etat* album-- her hair in a blonde Mohawk raising her fist in the air. Vedder has been photographed wearing this shirt on at least two occasions: onstage at the London Astoria and on the cover of a July 2006 issue of Rolling Stone. Vedder has also been photographed wearing a Plasmatics t-shirt with a head and shoulders image of Wendy and the phrase Wendy Will Win, from the poster for the fundraising shows at Bond's in New York, staged to drum up money for legal troubles that plagued Wendy.

Jack Osbourne, son of Ozzy and Sharon Osbourne, who appeared in the MTV reality show *The Osbournes*, has also been photographed wearing the Plasmatics "The Brainwashed…" t-shirt while running, with his hair cut in a Mohawk (one can imagine Wendy approving of this).

According to Kate Baudelaire, writing on the CVLT Nation Bizarre website in September of 2018, the UK press – always hungry for sensationalism and outrage – met Wendy at the airport when the Plasmatics were scheduled to perform at a sold-out debut show at London's Hammersmith Odeon on August 8, 1980. Two months before *New Hope For The Wretched*'s release in the US, and, as stated in *Be Stiff:The Stiff Records Story,* written by Richard Balls, *New Hope…*was to be released in the UK to coincide with this performance. Sensational headlines such as the aforementioned "Queen of Shock Rock," "Dominatrix of the Decibels," and "Evel Kneivel of Rock," were generated about Wendy. Wendy showed up at the airport in London dressed in a nurse's uniform. She told the reporters: "'I'm here to give a cultural enema to the British people."

"David Robinson was president of Stiff Records at the time so he brought us over," recalls Stu Deutsch, "They rented a house for us. I had been to London, I had relatives in London."

In an unusual bit of quasi brush–greatness trivia, Stu's London relatives owned the only grocery store in Paul McCartney's neighborhood. "I was Paul McCartney's grocery boy when I was 17," Stu says with a little laugh, "He would order all the time and I would deliver what he ordered. I never saw him in the house, though. I knew the maid, I saw the maid quite often. I did see Martha, the sheepdog who *(Beatles' song)* "Martha My Dear" was written about," he says.

In London, the Plasmatics rehearsed at Shepperton Studios, quite possibly the biggest film studio in England, known for its underwater stages and being the studios where James Bond movies were shot. "The Who had a section of Shepperton and we rehearsed at their studios," Stu recalls, adding "I was a huge Who fan, I'd seen them three dozen times, you know, Keith Moon, the whole thing."

The Plasmatics were planning to blow up a car onstage at the London Hammersmith Odeon concert. Stiff Records bought three cars for the Plasmatics and they did a test run for the Greater London Council, the local administrative government body for Greater London at the time.

"I remember we tested one and they said, 'no, never,' they weren't going to let us do it," Deutsch recalls. "They wanted a certain distance between the audience and the band," says Jean Beauvoir. "Roger Daltrey showed up when we blew up the car," says Deutsch, "he wasn't close to the explosion. He heard about it and he showed up to see the car blown up. The cars were blown up in a field outside the rehearsal studio.

"So the GLC came," Stu recalls, "they saw us blow up a car. We were supposed to play the Hammersmith Odeon, they saw us blow up a car and they said no and it was cancelled. They said, 'if you want to play and blow up the car we won't allow it.' And during that week

I had friends who were doing lights for Pink Floyd, who were just doing *The Wall* at that time, so I did go down there at one point and I saw the drummer and he said, 'Yeah, the GLC really doesn't let anybody do stuff.' The British bands get a bit of a break with pyrotechnics, like using the helicopter in The Wall, but even KISS-- they couldn't play in London proper, they had to play in Wembley or something like that to do their pyro properly."

Forbidden from performing a concert and blowing up a car in London the way they had been accustomed to in the United States, the Plasmatics held a press conference the next day. "The English press, you know, they're different," Stu says, "all they wanted was for Wendy to take her shirt off."

"I was heartbroken about the London show being cancelled," recalls Richie Stotts. "We were at a good point in the band. I feel like maybe it was a lost opportunity for the band. I think it still would have been a good show if we didn't blow up the car. I think we would have been good. I saw all the punk kids in the road. We were set up, we had done the sound check – it was like being an athlete when you're suited up and ready to play and all of a sudden the game is cancelled. That wasn't right. In hindsight it would have been great if the Plasmatics played."

Plasmatics toured Europe in 1981. They didn't go to Asia or South America. In Milan they walked into a riot between communists and fascists after one of their concerts, amid other adventures. "We played in Berlin and we had to drive through the corridor, I got caught speeding," Stotts recalls, referring to the days when the Berlin Wall was still dividing Germany. "You had to go through the checkpoints; first the Americans, then the West Germans, then the East Germans then the Russians. They catch you for speeding when you get to a checkpoint too soon, and Stu spoke German so he's talking to the guards in German. After our last show, which was in Berlin, we're in the car and we see all these kids walking away with our amps and stuff, like little ants."

As Wendy told music journalist Edouard Dauphin In the September, 1981 issue of *Creem*: "We went to Hamburg. The promoter told us beforehand: 'If they don't like you, they'll run you off the stage,' I said: 'No one runs us off the stage.' The show starts.

I look out into the audience and the place is filled with leather boys. Some of these guys were sixty years old! I mean these were not day trippers—they had leather up the ass! Then I notice this one leather boy right inform of the stage and he looks like the toughest one of all. He's orchestrating the whole group. He's controlling them, wielding a cat o' nine tails. They didn't bother us at all. We did a great show. I love being scared."

Plasmatics fan Lolo Martino had a boyfriend that was at the Plasmatics gig in Zurich, Switzerland "[It was] the only time when they've been thrown bottles on the stage by the audience and had to stop the concert in the middle of it. There was a very anti-American oriented punk scene at that time in the 80s, and at this particular time of the gig, the punks were really pissed off that the municipal authorities had closed their autonomous cultural center." "There was a riot in Zurich," Stotts adds, "that some rich person paid people to have a riot. We didn't get it. I didn't understand the politics."

"All our tours were insane," says Jean Beauvoir. "The Plasmatics had the most devoted fans. We had everything from shotguns, chickens coming out of the ceiling (which were very well taken care of by the way) blowing up cars on stage, exploding amplifiers, chain sawing guitars, breaking up TV sets and just the sheer energy of the performance. The main element and what I believe the attraction was that the show was unpredictable--you never knew what could or would or may happen on any given night. How high would the exploding car hood go - 75 ft, 50 or 25?"

"I had an amazing time traveling the world and blowing things up on stage for Wendy," says Peter Cappadocia (also known as Pyro Pete) who was in charge of pyrotechnics for the Plasmatics. "She was great to work with as she understood that what we were doing was dangerous and she would always be on her mark on stage. She was always double checking and asking questions at safety meetings before a show where we blew up a car. She wanted to give the fans the best show possible."

New Hope For The Wretched did chart in the UK and the single, "Butcher Baby" charted up to number 55 in the UK singles rankings. Although the Plasmatics' debut got little radio airplay in the U.S. and peaked at number 134 on the *Billboard* Album Chart on March

21,1981, word of mouth about the Plasmatics' outrageous exploits garnered them a substantial following among punk rock fans.

In a video for "Butcher Baby," Wendy is topless except for what seems to be clothespins on her nipples and shaving cream smeared on her breasts. Black electrical tape is wound around her bare legs and she is wearing sand-colored underwear and a black leather cap on her head. In the opening shot, she raises her fist in the air and growls: "Butcher baby/They're going to put you away!" The other band members onstage with Wendy wear full hood-type masks covering their heads.

Wendy chainsaws a guitar in half, sticking out her tongue as if destroying the guitar is a sexually pleasurable act. Once the guitar is cut into two pieces, she holds the sawed-off neck triumphantly in the air. At the end of the song, Wendy is presented with a console, she flips the switches and the speakers explode. Wendy holds her arms up amid this wreckage, in a gesture of victory.

As of April 2020, this video for "Butcher Baby" video had over two million views on You Tube. "Butcher Baby" went on to become an anthem for the Plasmatics; one of their most recognized songs. In an interview with *People* Magazine circa 1981, Wendy mentioned having orgasms onstage when she performed, specifically when she sang "Butcher Baby."

On the German music television show *Musik Laden*, the Plasmatics perform their cover of the early Sixties Bobby Darin hit "Dream Lover," also a song on *New Hope For The Wretched*. Wendy is wearing her leopard-print leotard that leaves her breasts exposed. She is wearing black tape on her nipples and a black underwire bra that has no cups.

On stage left there's a white Mercedes-Benz. Wendy picks up a sledgehammer and smashes the headlights. Wendy sits on the hood of the car, folding her right leg. She sings the lyrics – about wanting a dream lover to cure her loneliness as she briefly caresses her left breast and gingerly touches her genital area hinting at masturbation. By pairing these lyrics with these gestures, Wendy is shining a spotlight on a taboo subject. It's safe to say that probably everyone has masturbated at least once in their life but it's not discussed in polite society. People also perhaps imagine a dream lover when masturbating as well.

Soon after *New Hope ForThe Wretched*'s release, the staff at St. Marks Sounds, a venerable record store in New York's East Village, tacked a Plasmatics poster, featuring Wendy in a revealing striped top and a miniskirt exposing her underwear, on a wall right near the shop's entrance. It was the first thing many customers saw upon entering the store. The poster remained on that wall until St. Marks Sounds closed in 2014.

In January 1981, the Plasmatics were musical guests on an episode of *Fridays* – ABC-TV's late night Los Angeles-based sketch comedy show positioned to compete with NBC's iconic *Saturday Night Live*. *Fridays* was known for having top-notch musical guests with an underground cachet– The Jam, The Clash, DEVO and others.
By appearing on Fridays, Wendy became the first woman on national TV to wear her hair in a Mohawk.

As a *Fridays* cast member doing an imitation of Lawrence Welk introduces the Plasmatics, there's a rumbling of anticipation coming from the audience. After he refers to "sweet little Wendy O. Williams" and then says "Ladies and gentlemen – the Plasmatics!" the camera focuses on Wendy sporting her black and blonde Mohawk, a tank top tee shirt bearing the handwritten phrase "DON'T BE A WANKER!" (ABC-TV censors were concerned that Wendy's nipples would be visible through her clingy tee shirt and had her tape her nipples down with masking tape), red pants with black tape wound around her legs and black fringed white booties.

She growls into her microphone a rallying cry: "Ok America turn up your TV set!" As the Plasmatics kick into "The Living Dead." Richie stands next to Wendy and he's wearing a tweaked French maid outfit with a white tutu. Wendy sings with a palpable growl.

A 1950's TV set that looks like it was taken straight from the set of *The Adventures of Ozzie and Harriet* is brought to the stage and turned on. Wendy gestures with her arms, presenting the TV to the audience, as if to say "Behold! Here is the false god you're worshipping!" She then grabs a large axe from the drum riser and hacks away at the TV, smashing it to pieces as it blows up.

Ronald Reagan was going to be inaugurated as President in a few days, sold to the American people partly via his "Morning in America" television commercial. "I tried to warn you/I tried to stop you" Wendy emphatically snarls amid the wreckage of the TV like Cassandra warning her audience of a "future" where they'll be staring at a screen all the time.

For Wendy and the Plasmatics, being a musical guest on *Fridays* was a chance to subvert the medium of television – and what better way to do so than destroy a TV while they were *on* television?

At the time of the Plasmatics' *Fridays* appearance, MTV hadn't established itself yet as a conduit for generating substantial record sales. Therefore an appearance as a musical guest on a late-night nationally broadcast comedy show like *Fridays* or *Saturday Night Live* could certainly be a coveted opportunity for a band that wants to sell records (something it's assumed all recording artists want to do). In their performance on *Fridays*, chaos and mayhem seemed to be the Plasmatics's agenda instead of going gold or platinum.

When the Plasmatics return for their second song on *Fridays*, they are introduced by another cast member who acts terrified as he cowers and says, "Once again—The Plaaasssmmaatics!"

This time Wendy is wearing white briefs and a black bra, her chest area is smeared with shaving cream and she sports a black leather cap as she starts to sing "Butcher Baby." Jean Beauvoir is in his trademark white tux and a dark blue executioner's hood. Richie Stotts is dressed like a demented Playboy bunny. Wendy punctuates the lyrics of "Butcher Baby" by emphatically uttering "Uhh!" as a guttural refrain.

The camera next shows Wendy cutting apart an expensive-looking electric guitar with a chainsaw. She cuts apart the guitar with slow, deep strokes as she sticks out her tongue, making the act appear sexual – as if she's pleasing the guitar as she's rendering it useless. She then runs to the audience and hands them pieces of the guitar.

Since the late sixties "guitar heroes" were deified male figures in the rock music pantheon: Jimi Hendrix, Pete Townshend, Jimmy Page, Keith Richards, to name a few. For Wendy, being a woman fronting a band, hacking apart the favorite toy of worshipped boy rock stars was a subversive, feminist act that was very punk rock. Johnny Rotten snarlingly drawled the word "destroy" at the end of the Sex Pistols' "Anarchy In The U.K." but he was just talking the talk – Wendy *actually* destroyed the instrument at the heart of rock culture, as if to nullify the concept of the typically male rock icon.

Even though Townshend and The Who destroyed their instruments at the end of many a performance in the Sixties, by the Seventies that had become schtick --schtick that would be dusted off and decontextualized in the early Nineties by Nirvana. Finding themselves unwittingly spearheading the grunge phenomenon, Nirvana put a post-modern, more self-immolating spin on the act of destroying instruments, doing so in a scorched -earth policy manner.

Being rather dismayed about his multi-platinum success, in interviews Kurt Cobain made it clear he didn't want to be a cliched guitar superstar.

Conversely, singer/songwriter John Hiatt, chagrined by guitar destruction, wrote and recorded the song "Perfectly Good Guitars," lamenting how certain rock musicians demolished instruments he regarded as precious.

Despite being a Plasmatics' lead guitarist, Stotts didn't take umbrage at Wendy's tearing apart the instrument he played.

"There was a store called 48th Street Guitars, they sold only used guitars," replies Richie Stotts when asked about Wendy's guitar destruction. "So we'd get cheap guitars from there. Richie Friedman there had a bunch of Gibson stickers, he gave us a wad of them. So before a show we'd take some cheap Korean guitar, get a little spray paint, cover up the cheap guitar name and put on the Gibson sticker. People went nuts, writing in to *Rolling Stone* about us tearing up Gibson guitars. A lot of people took the pickups and pieces and put them in their guitars. We just took it one step further. I thought that was one of the best props we had, it worked out well."

At the end of the Plasmatics' performance on *Fridays* of "Butcher Baby"–which had become the band's anthem by this time, Wendy – after saying , "Good night! We love you!" fires a shotgun at the speakers, which then blow up, then she fires the gun at the lighting rig above the stage, which comes crashing down.

"Would Wendy miss and shoot somebody with that shotgun?" Remarked Jean Beauvoir in 2019, "Yes it has happened, though it was blanks it's still pretty painful," he said.

"Wendy shot me with a shotgun loaded with blanks once," says Richie Stotts, "I still have the scar on my leg. I also have scars from people biting my leg, laying in TV glass which has a coating that's very infective."

"Wendy was great on stage with handling the chainsaw and the shotgun," Pete Cappadocia recalls, "which was a real shotgun that I would load with blanks, but still very dangerous, a blank to the face from 3 feet away would still kill a person. I was in charge of the chainsaw, the sledge hammer, and all the pyro. In the beginning when we were playing clubs it was a different stage every night and the pyro would be very close to her and the other band members some times. She was always aware of where it was and where her safe zones where. We blew up lots of things and no one was ever hurt."

As the Plasmatics leave the *Fridays* set, the camera turns to the audience and shows that they're mostly teenage punk rockers. They stand up and cheer wildly, many waving *New Hope For The Wretched* album flats.

Most radio stations ignored the Plasmatics, but LA's KROQ— regarded for playing new wave bands-- was *somewhat* supportive of them. At one point, KROQ sponsored a contest where the winner won a brand new TV set and the Plasmatics would come to their house and destroy their old television set. According to Star666, writing on the GossipELA website, reflecting back on this contest: "...the band's affinity for smashing stuff caught the eye of LA radio station KROQ, which launched a contest for their listeners although the band was in town to execute a series of sold-out shows about Southern California. At least one particular fortunate winner won a new television set from KROQ, who then had the pleasure of getting Williams to smash up their old TV on their front lawn." It would have been more subversive if the contest had the Plasmatics demolished the winner's old TV set and left it at that, though it probably would have been hard for the station to find contest entrants in the Los Angeles/Pasadena vicinity willing to give up their television altogether. The contest winner had their TV sledgehammered by Wendy on June 16, 1981.

At this time, the presence of young people in the Los Angeles music scene was markedly different than the older music crowd in New York. In *Making Tracks: The Rise of Blondeie* (written by Debbie Harry, Chris Stein and renowned rock biographer Victor Bockris) about perhaps the most commercially successful band to emerge from the late Seventies CBGB scene, Debbie Harry remarks that when Blondeie went to Los Angeles for the first time, they were "surprised at how many teenagers" they encountered at their concerts, etc. Chalk that up maybe partly to liquor laws being a bit more lax in LA – where everyone has to drive, thus perhaps less people at gigs would be drinking alcoholic beverages-- and clubs might not have been as stringent about checking IDs at the door as they were in New York.

"There was a party after *Fridays* at someone's house that was a great party," Stotts recalls as he reminisces about how the Plasmatics were embraced in Los Angeles. "When we played The Whiskey A-Go-Go it was incredible. We were really accepted out there in L.A., they were more open to us, they loved us. There was no judgment. Me and Wes went to this giant huge disco. We were ushered into a VIP room and they played "Monkey Suit," and everyone was going nuts."

Christine Hadlow, a music fan from Queens, New York, was just entering her tween years and discovering punk when the Plasmatics emerged. She describes what it was like to witness a performance by Wendy and be shaken up by her presence even through the "safe" medium of TV: "Wendy was fierce, raw, angry and scary. The first time I saw her was on *Fridays*," Hadlow says. "I was 11 or 12. I had very 'outer borough' sensibilities and I saw this and it was so raw, powerful and terrifying. I was overwhelmed. I was frightened by her. I felt scared and threatened. I didn't like the music-- it was too chaotic and it didn't make any sense to me. It was chaos and cacophony. And I remember looking at her with the Mohawk. She was in great shape, she was obviously very disciplined with her body. She dressed very scantily but there was nothing sexy or feminine about her."

Hadlow continues to describe being somewhat perplexed and disturbed by Wendy: "I saw she was a persona more than a person. She had that tough hard edge and to me it wasn't about the music it was more like performance art. Music was almost secondary -- it was more like spectacle. It was jarring. As a kid I had trouble sleeping because it was so jarring. That was the point of the Plasmatics.

(New York City UHF music video channel) U68 had the metal power hour and the Plasmatics were on it. I heard their music but it never moved me. But I'll never forget Wendy O. Williams," Hadlow concludes, "It's kind of like how Andy Kaufman never told jokes-- to me she never sang. In the genres of metal and hard rock she's an icon but there was nothing musical about it."

In contrast to how radio had very little interest in broadcasting the Plasmatics' music, television appearances worked very well for them, possibly because the Plasmatics were extremely visual. Each member had a distinct look and they were fronted by Wendy who gave new definition to the term "blonde bombshell." The chaos that ensued when they destroyed things as part of their performances truly made them a band that had to be seen to be believed.

The Plasmatics made the most of being on TV. Aside from their groundbreaking appearance on *Fridays,* the Plasmatics appeared on *Tomorrow* with Tom Snyder twice in 1981. "We did the *Tomorrow* show twice because the ratings were so high," says Jean Beauvoir. On their first appearance, Snyder introduced them as "possibly the greatest punk band in the world," Wendy smashed a TV with a sledge hammer and cut up an electric guitar with a chainsaw.

When the Plasmatics appeared on *Tomorrow* for the second time in May of 1981. Incidentally the disco song "Relight My Fire" by Dan Hartman – who would later produce the Plasmatics' *Metal Priestess* EP – was the theme song for the *Tomorrow* show. Wendy was dressed like a Catholic schoolgirl, in a plaid skirt, white blouse and knee socks. The center part of her Mohawk is dyed black. She walks down the steps through the excited audience to the stage where, as the band rips into "Headbanger," Wendy throws a large vase of flowers to the floor.

In the *Tomorrow* show audience that night was Mike Schnapp, a Plasmatics fan in his late teens at the time of the second Plasmatics appearance. Schnapp was the winner of a contest sponsored by pioneering Long Island radio station WLIR. He described the contest in a 2020 interview: "25 people won a copy of the Plasmatics second album *Beyond The Valley of 1984*, five people won tickets to see them at Bond's and the grand prize winner got the album, Bond's tickets and a pair of tickets to the Plasmatics' appearance on the *Tomorrow* show with Tom Snyder. I won the whole thing! The album, Bond's tickets and the Tom Snyder tickets! I was so thrilled! The Bond's show was absolutely fantastic and then I went to see the Tom Snyder show," he recalled.

Aside from the Plasmatics, another guest on *Tomorrow* that night was televangelist Rex Humbard, host of a religious TV show called *You Are Loved*. "I don't think there were very many people in the audience for him," Schnapp recalled.

One might think that Wendy and Humbard would have clashed in the green room of *Tomorrow* but no. Wendy's fabled politeness and charm made for a pleasant encounter. "Rex was alright," Wendy remarked to Edouard Dauphin during an interview for *Creem* magazine the day after the Plasmatics' second appearance on *Tomorrow*. "I went up to him before the taping and said 'Rex, you are loved.' He said, 'You are loved too, Wendy. I think what you're doing is great.' He gave me a You Are Loved pin. Then he looked at what I was wearing and said, 'I don't know where you're going to put it.' This guy's on a great trip!"

Wendy is constantly moving on the *Tomorrow* set as the Plasmatics play "Headbanger." She shimmies onstage, running around to and fro. Her plaid pleated skirt is very short and as she shakes her hips, her neutral colored panties are visible at times. Her schoolgirl outfit is more modest than her trademark black tape and shaving cream on her breasts, but is still provocative. In the lexicon of what heterosexual men typically find sexy, a teenage girl in a school uniform is a common fantasy, but Wendy being dressed this way, with her black and blonde Mohawk and fierce vocals, yanks that image out of the male gaze.

Tomorrow was on NBC, a major commercial television network. It's plausible that Wendy's electrical tape and shaving cream wouldn't be approved by that network's censors.

Richie Stotts, wearing a two-piece studded black leather outfit, runs into the crowd as he plays his Flying Vee guitar. He leans back against seated studio audience members and then falls on some others in a lower row, who are clearly enjoying the spectacle. Many audience members are cheering, some holding up handmade signs. Jean Beauvoir is playing keyboards, wearing his white tuxedo. Wes Beech is clad in a black suit and white shirt with his customary football player's black marking under his eyes.

"So I was there in the studio and at one point you see Richie Stotts run into the audience and then he runs down one of the aisles," says Mike Schnapp. "He ran down my aisle and he stepped on my foot! And I was jumping up and down like 'yeaaahh!' I was so psyched! And then he falls down a couple of rows…it was mayhem. I'd never seen this before. I'd been in a couple of live studio audiences before. I'd been seeing concerts since I was about 13 and it had to be the craziest thing I'd ever seen on so many levels."

As the song ends, Wendy shouts "You're a headbanger!" over and over with her fist in the air. It's not clear if Wendy's putting down headbangers or asking them to pledge allegiance to her and the Plasmatics. Maybe both?

Being on *Tomorrow* gave Wendy an opportunity to speak for herself and espouse her philosophy as well as perform with her band and promote them. When Wendy sat for her interview with Tom Snyder (who had a reputation for being punchy and rancorous), she was smiling and brightly alert, with her knees pulled up to her chest. Before the interview, a female voice in the audience shouts, "We love you Wendy!" Snyder hushes the crowd by saying, "Yes, yes, Wendy loves you too."

Snyder asks Wendy about the reasons behind the Plasmatics destroying big ticket consumer items. Wendy responds: "It's normal for rape and murder to happen in our society but it's not normal to destroy a television set. We're exorcising the evil in our society by destroying these things."

Speaking about Wendy's penchant for destruction, Snyder then suggests Wendy should "slow things down a bit," and the audience collectively and loudly shouts *"No!"*

As Maria Raha states in the *Wendy O. Williams 10 years of Revolutionary Rock and Roll* documentary: "When the Plasmatics were getting a lot of television exposure and mainstream exposure, the eighties were getting steeped in capitalistic greed. She stood in direct opposition to all the things people were buying into. Her decimating those symbols was really striking a chord with people who bought into that mindset and thought they were fulfilling themselves by buying big-ticketed items."

"Materialism is rampant," Wendy goes on to say in this second *Tomorrow* show appearance, "you've just got to flush it down the toilet. We've got to undermine the status quo. When you hold on and repress things, out comes the violence."

Snyder asks how long Wendy has wanted to destroy things and she replies, "I've been like this all my life. I can't help but do what I feel and encourage people to do what they feel. I get a release and a relief from when I do these things and my band gets a release and a relief too."

She goes on to say, "Everybody should have this opportunity because when you hold stuff in and suppress things you get more violence. Out of this boredom come the assassins and the real sickies."

Snyder suggests she stop destroying things. Wendy laughs and says, "Oh Tom, you've got to let me have my fun!" As they cut to a commercial, Wendy hugs Snyder.

The Plasmatics come back again after a commercial break. Wendy is clad in a black bra, black vinyl pants and boots with a substantial heel. They launch into "Masterplan." Wendy sings the word "masterplan" in a high-pitched quasi shout, alternately singing the verses of the song in a lower register. Richie, again clad in a black leather and metal studded outfit and sporting his trademark blue Mohawk, runs through the audience during the song's bridge, shredding notes on his Flying Vee guitar. Jean Beauvoir wears his white suit and an American flag-motifed motorcycle helmet, Wes Beech is wearing a black suit, white socks and white sneakers.

There's an orange Chevy Nova on stage right. This make of car was one of the greatest marketing blunders in the history of the auto industry. Chevrolet executives didn't realize that translated into Spanish, the word Nova means "*no va*" – *won't go*. Not exactly the kind of aspirational branding the automaker hoped would sell a lot of cars.

Wendy shakes up a can of black spray paint and sprays the word FORNICATE on the doors of the passenger side of the Nova -- during concerts she'd spray paint FUCK on cars but that certainly wouldn't get past the NBC censors - and THE STATUS QUO on the hood of the car. She grabs a sledgehammer and smashes the windshield and headlights of the car. Wendy extracts the rearview mirror and pair of fuzzy dice from the car and hands them to an audience member who accepts them with both hands.

Then Wendy is holding dynamite which a man in a lab coat lights up. Wendy then parades the explosive with its very long lit fuse in front of the cheering audience as if it's sage she's purifying the studio with. Then she throws it in the side window of the car. She moves away and the car explodes. Men in white lab coats then douse the destroyed car with fire extinguishers. The audience applauds and cheers what may very well have been the Chevy Nova's sole moment of glory--although at a Plasmatics concert at Perkins Palace in Pasadena, California in June of 1981, Wendy also smashes the windshield of another orange Chevy Nova and blows that up too.

"During "Masterplan" they blew the car up," says Mike Schnapp. "It was just crazy; the whole studio shook! That was no joke. They threw dynamite in there. You gotta think that after that show the network must have thought, "we can't let this happen anymore," because it was really… it wasn't like 'boom', whatever. The *whole studio shook*. The hood blew upward, things were flying all over. I've seen thousands of shows, hundreds of thousands of bands since the mid-Seventies and that was the craziest performance I ever saw, " he recalls.

How did the studio audience react? Schnapp says: "For a second it was like '*holy shit!*' and then everyone was like '*Yeaaah!*' it got everyone crazy, everyone was psyched. I don't know how many people were there to see the minster or priest but it seemed like the whole crowd was there for the Plasmatics. Just being in a TV studio where it's very quiet and respectful and then all of a sudden this stuff happens! Seeing this happen at a rock concert is one thing but seeing it in a TV studio is just off the hook! One of those most memorable things in my life."

SCTV was a Toronto-based ensemble sketch comedy television show centered around a fictional television network. On *The Fishin' Musician* segment, SCTV cast member John Candy, playing a character named Gil Fisher, proprietor of The Scuttlebutt Lodge, calls the Plasmatics "The greatest band there is." When the Plasmatics appeared on the show in 1981, the band and Candy go on a "photo safari" where Wendy attacks a guy in a gorilla suit who comes out of a cave. Wendy mentions their EP *Metal Priestess* and they perform "Doom Song" as Wendy wears her headband with its rhino horn. She also wears a midriff top with leather crosses on her breasts that cover her nipples but expose the rest of her breasts. Wendy didn't want to wear something else although studio officials threatened to cancel the Plasmatics' SCTV appearance if she didn't. Wendy was convinced by one of the show's makeup artists to have her breasts painted black and the show went on.

The Plasmatics are very metal in the performance segment of their appearance – there's a pentagram as a backdrop, Richie wearing a black leather pointy shouldered vest, Wes Beech in vampire garb. Wendy then proceeds to smash the contents of the Scuttlebutt Lodge – TV, vases, windows-- and returns to the mic as fog envelops the stage. John Candy is delighted amid the wreckage.

The Plasmatics performed on *Solid Gold*, the syndicated pop music countdown TV show later in 1981. There's something rather surreal about watching the show's Top 40-pedestrian hosts, Fifth Dimension singer Marilyn McCoo and former teen idol and youngest brother to the Bee Gees, Andy Gibb introduce the Plasmatics' as "one of the most original and controversial bands on the music scene today" and "never boring" (damning with faint praise there?).

The Plasmatics' performance begins with Wendy walking to the stage through the audience holding bunches of gladiolas and tossing them to the crowd. She is wearing a black leather midriff top that looks similar to the one that she wore on SCTV, black bikini bottoms, black boots and her headband with a rhino horn protruding from it.

The Plasmatics don't so much perform on the *Solid Gold* set as *invade* it as they kick into "Black Leather Monster." Musically speaking, they're far more noisy and aggressive than the other radio-friendly artists who appeared on that show. Wendy mounts a guitar on a sawhorse, saws it in half and hands the neck and sliced half of the guitar's body to people in the audience. Wendy constantly moves as she growls the lyrics to the song.

In a March 09, 2016 article by Courtney Devores in *The Charlotte Observer*, Cee-Lo Green, singer for Gnarls Barkley, reflected on how influenced he was by seeing this Plasmatics performance:

"When I was a kid – I'm not sure what year – I may have been 3 or 4 or 5 or 6. But I was watching *Solid Gold* hosted by Marilyn McCoo. the Plasmatics and Wendy O. Williams were performing," remembers Green. Watching the November 1981 clip on YouTube, it's evident the infamously controversial Plasmatics, with Williams shouting and growling in a leather bikini and knee-high boots, was unlike anything on the Top 40-based series at the time. CeeLo was attracted to the image of Williams' blonde Mohawk.

"As long as I can remember, I always wanted a Mohawk. She had a headpiece with a horn in the forehead," he adds. "I thought this was such an awesome contradiction to the straight-laced staging of 'Solid Gold.' It just got at me. As long as I can remember my first love was punk rock music."

After performing "Black Leather Monster," and in marked contrast to the chaos enveloping the *Solid Gold* stage mere seconds before, Wendy exchanges reserved-yet-game banter with Madam, Wayland Flowers's elderly faded glamour girl ventriloquist puppet. Madam's hair is coiffed in an ersatz Mohawk with bursts of spray-on color and Wendy asks Madam where she got her hair done as if they're old girlfriends. In their conversation, Wendy has an aura of calm in marked contrast to the intense way she had just performed onstage with the Plasmatics. As Wendy stands with her hand on her hip Madam says to her: "So, I hear sometimes you blow up cars in your concerts..."

To which Wendy matter-of-factly quips: "Some-times…sometimes that's true, when I sing a love song." At the end of Wendy's chat with Madam, Wendy blows a kiss to the audience.

"I left in '81," says drummer Stu Deutsch. "My last show was the day before Reagan was shot. I remember the next day I saw Hinckley and all that stuff. I promised I would do the first TV show, so I did the *Tomorrow* show with Tom Snyder. Jean Beauvoir left a month after me," says Deutsch of his departure from the Plasmatics in 1981.

"Richie left about a year later and that was pretty much the end of it. None of us were making any money; yeah we were playing shows, people knew about us but there wasn't much money.

"I went to Los Angeles about a month after I quit," says Deutsch, "I had friends out there. I talked to Rod and he said "This is not a good time, we're doing the second album," and I said, 'Well we never saw much money from the first,' so it didn't make much sense doing the second one."

"So our original contracts – it was me, Richie, Chosei and Wendy – we had signed up for three years and the three years was up. We had these new massive contracts and I was never signing that. Wes and Richie signed it but Jean and I weren't signing the second one.

"When I went to LA I played with a lot of people, the most notable was Johnette Napolitano and Jim from Concrete Blondee, we were called the L.A. Dreamers. I'm still really good friends with Johnette, she calls up whenever she's in town."

At the time of our conversation in 2019, Deutsch was playing drums with musician friends – "Richie and I did do a couple of shows with Blue Coop – the Blue Oyster Cult and Alice Cooper guys—we did an autograph session and a few songs with them." As for how he currently earns a living, Deutsch's line of work has more than a hint of irony:

"Let's just say it's the opposite of what I did in the Plasmatics – I'm involved in safety, I deal with OSHA, *(the US government's occupational safety and hazards administration)* stuff like that. You can say I'm doing penance for what I did in the Plasmatics - I'm a safety manager."

In 1981, Stiff Records was eager to release a second Plasmatics album to capitalize on the interest generated by *New Hope For The Wretched* and the media appearances and publicity surrounding the Plasmatics' debut for the label.

After the departure of Stu Deutsch, Neal Smith – Alice Cooper's drummer-- played drums for the Plasmatics on their second album, *Beyond the Valley of 1984*.

"The Plasmatics changed music more than The Stooges ever did," Smith reflected in a 2019 interview.

Smith saw the Plasmatics for the first time circa 1979/1980 at the Oxford Ale House in New Haven, Connecticut. He had heard a lot about the band.

At that time, Smith was also in a band called the Flying Tigers who had played at the Oxford Ale House and he knew the owners of the venue. "I was very impressed," he says of seeing the Plasmatics for the first time, "The whole vibe was 100% Plasmatics. The guitar that was mounted on a sawhorse…When they came on they blew me away, Wendy had the back tape on her nipples, the white Mohawk, Richie had the blue that was just a comfortable level of how they were. The songs were just a whole other level of punk, their songs were just edgy and catchy and fresh, that's always a great thing to see."

Smith wanted to meet the band. "I knew one of their roadies and he introduced me to them. I was so impressed with how they owned the stage. It was just a pub in New Haven but they were the real deal." Smith had a burning question for the Plasmatics. Coming from his baby boomer perspective, the biggest influence on him in terms of albums was The Beatles' *Sergeant Pepper's Lonely Hearts Club Band*. "So I said, 'What record was the biggest influence on the Plasmatics?' Without skipping a beat they said '*Pretties For You*, the first Alice Cooper Group album; that is our *Sgt. Pepper*.' I was blown away by that! I said no wonder you guys are so fucking crazy," he laughs. "That was the most sincere compliment. I said 'I don't make this offer often' but I gave them my number and said 'If you ever need a drummer, please get in touch with me.' About a year later I heard from Rod Swenson's office and they asked me to play on their next album, which was *Beyond the Valley of 1984*."

"I was living in Connecticut so I would take the train to New York City," Smith recalls, "and then take the subway to their rehearsal space in SoHo – and I never take the subway," explains Smith. "We rehearsed for a couple of weeks, then did the album in three weeks. I asked to keep my name very small on the album as I was going through a difficult divorce." (Smith also does not appear on the album's cover photo.)

"They were very focused, all business," Smith says, "No one even cracked open a beer during rehearsal. Everyone was very professional, we didn't party together, it was a business. I spent a lot of time with Jean Beauvoir who was also a great drummer and he'd show me the groove of the songs. Wendy was great, very professional. Playing those songs was quite a workout. They worked extremely hard. They were the real deal, I give them kudos for that."

Beyond the Valley of 1984 was produced by Rod Swenson who came up with the title, even though the album was recorded and released in May *1981*. Always casting a critical eye on the poisoned aspects of the world around them, the title of this album may have been warning of the onset of Big Brother, thought-crime, doublespeak and a status quo determined to convince everyone that 2+2=5. Or perhaps Plasmatics were offering the listener a type of rescue from an Orwellian world they were already living in yet might not be aware of.

The album's title is similar to Russ Meyers's films such as *Beyond The Valley of the Dolls*, a 1970 cult film depicting Hollywood music scene debauchery and Meyers's cheesecake opus *Beneath the Valley of the Ultravixens*, known for its cast of voluptuous actresses. Though not having too much in common with Meyers's sexploitation films, this album's title insinuates that the listener will experience something quite removed from their everyday experience.

The cover image of *Beyond The Valley of 1984* is compelling: Wendy, Wes Beech, Jean Beauvoir and Richie Stotts, each on horseback with their fists in the air in front of a giant cactus photographed in the Arizona desert. Wendy is wearing a black leather jacket with nothing underneath except electrical tape on her nipples. Her hair is styled in a black Mohawk with the sides of her hair blonde. The four members of the Plasmatics pictured here on horseback are a warning force; the four horsemen of the apocalypse - led by a woman heralding a toxic society's impending doom. The album's art also features an image of a white Cadillac blowing up surrounded by gas mask-wearing men in white lab coats as a helicopter hovers close by.

The album opens with the sound of a heavy bell leading into "Incantation," where the band chants "omni maximus Plasmaticum" ominously. Loosely translated that means "all things greatest in the world of the Plasmatics." Incantations often signal the beginning of a ritual or rite – something supernatural about to happen.

"Masterplan,"(with its very punk count off of "1-2,1-2 fuck you") boldly finds Wendy name checking Superman, a macho man, a delivery man and the Klu Klux Klan as she insists "you had it made/but you blew it," holding men -- some in power, some less so- - accountable. Wendy's vocals on "Headbanger" practically purr:

"You got a special skill/Headbanger/you live for overkill/ you know how to get your chills/you know how to get your thrills." The song ends with Wendy shouting "You're a headbanger!" again in a manner that's ambiguous as to whether she's celebrating or castigating said person banging their head. Maybe they're an obsessive music fan or someone being sadly self-destructive? Or maybe both?

Rod Swenson, Wes Beech, Richie Stotts and Jean Beauvoir have songwriting credits on *Beyond The Valley of 1984*. Recorded at The Ranch in New York City, Rod Swenson and the Plasmatics are listed as having production credits.

"Summer Nite" is a vignette of a night out that takes a violent turn and goes very wrong. Its lyrics are sung in a narrative style by Wendy and it seems not a million miles away from early-Sixties girl-group tragedy songs like the Shangri-Las "Leader Of The Pack" and "Walking In The Sand." In that vein, it's not surprising to find that "Summer Nite" features backup singing by the female vocal group The Angels, famous for their early Sixties hit "My Boyfriend's Back." The chorus The Angels sing opens with the words "baby baby" similar to a lot of the lyrics of pop songs of that girl group's heyday. Angels member Peggy Santiglia Ricker recalls about recording their vocals:

"We did it in a NYC studio. Only a few necessary people were there. A rather nondescript situation. Wendy was not there or I would have certainly remembered. Even the backup was super simple just some lines in unison."

As Wendy sings "Nothing" she brays "you aint got no nothing" throughout the song; a triple negative seemingly about a dead end personality—someone too afraid or inept to do anything. From the tone of her singing Wendy thinks this person is very contemptible.

Wendy's rapid-fire vocals on "Fast Food Service" speak in the voice of a woman in a couple deciding to get cheap food instead of having sex ("If going all the way ain't right/honey let's eat out tonight/fast food service"). The song has a hyper-quick rhythm that's almost humorous.

As *New Hope For The Wretched* had a song that was recorded live, *Beyond The Valley of 1984* has "Hitman," which was recorded live at a concert in Milan, Italy. A chant of Wendy's name opens the track and she enthusiastically greets the audience by shouting "Ciao Milano!" The song tells a hitman who he is and what he does --"You really knock 'em dead" is the song's refrain. The other live track on the album – "Plasma Jam," an instrumental also recorded in Milan. The sound of a roaring crowd is heard shortly after the song begins.

"Living Dead" appears both on Beyond the *Valley of 1984* and *New Hope For the Wretched*. On *Beyond.*.the song begins with the Plasmatics's signature countoff of "1-2 fuck you." There's a rather lengthy instrumental section and ends as Wendy makes guttural noises almost as if she's vomiting - made sick by the TV zombies she's singing about and taking to task.

"A Pig Is A Pig," starts with an uncharacteristically country-flavored preamble where Wendy dedicates the song to "the kind of person hiding under a guise of respectability," name checking a "cowardly" journalist "exploiting people who can't fight back", the assassin and "the sickie sadist who hides behind his police badge to commit crimes of violence against other people." The country flavored- intro is quickly jettisoned as Wendy, in full battle cry mode proclaims "Because a pig is a pig/ and that's that!" After a quick count off of "Ichi ni san shi," the ferocity the Plasmatics are renowned for bears its sonic fangs and bites deep.

Something notable about the songs on *Beyond The Valley of 1984* is how unlike most women singers topping the charts of that time by singing odes to male figures – whether they were Pat Benatar telling a guy to "Hit Me With Your Best Shot," Debby Boone setting number one hit single records with "You Light Up My Life," (A song Boone has said she was singing to God -- you can't get more goody two shoes than that), or Olivia Newton-John wanting to get "Physical" with a man she desires. Wendy is not singing about herself and her emotions towards a male object of her affection, but rather she's castigating various types of people (mostly male) who she finds appalling, specifically on "Masterplan," "Nothing," "A Pig is A Pig" and "Living Dead." Her ire is in full firepower on "Sex Junkie" where she describes how vile she finds her supplicant who is addicted to sex. At the end of the song she commands, "eat me!" demanding pleasure from this awful person who can't get enough.

In *Trouser Press*, critic Jim Green follows up his review of *New Hope For The Wretched* – were he calls the album "barely listenable" - by saying "*Beyond the Valley of 1984*, though, *is* quite listenable, if only intermittently memorable. Swenson's lyrics aspire to nightmares of apocalypse and superhuman lust and degradation. The music is likewise heavier, but clearer and not without flashes of finesse: punchy drums (courtesy of guest Neal Smith, once of the Alice Cooper ensemble), good guitar squeals from Swenson's main writing collaborator, Richie Stotts, and even a culture-shock backing-vocals appearance by the girl-group Angels."

At this time, musician/producer Dan Hartman had produced recordings by .38 Special and James Brown. He had hits himself with the disco songs "Instant Replay" and "Relight My Fire," (later on he would record the hit Motown-flavored R&B song "I Can Dream About You" from the soundtrack of the early '80s film *Streets of Fire*). He was intrigued by the Plasmatics upon hearing *Beyond The Valley of 1984* while working on a recording session in Los Angeles. Soon after, in 1981, he met with Wendy and Rod Swenson in New York. About a month later he and Swenson were producing what would become the Plasmatics' *Metal Priestess* EP at Hartman's former schoolhouse turned home and recording studio in Connecticut.

The cover art of *Metal Priestess* is quite "full metal" with a photo of Wendy standing in front of a large black pentagram – perhaps a nod to how Satanic imagery is popular in heavy metal - and clad in a midriff leather top that exposes her breasts (her nipples are covered with black and metal pasties). Her arm is extended and her hand points forward to a point above her head. Wendy's hair is a blonde Mohawk with her natural brown hair on the sides as her rhino horn headband wraps around her head. She is wearing knee high lace up high heeled boots and what appears to be a black leather thong.

On the back cover of *Metal Priestess*, Wes Beech is wearing a bluish-black cape with a high collar as he stands in front of a MOOG keyboard holding a lit black candle in his right hand. His trademark football player's black is under his eyes.

Richie Stotts is on the back cover too, his hair in a blue Mohawk and there's red lipstick and black eyeliner on his face. As he holds a blue electric guitar he is wearing a leather outfit that laces up the front with metal-tipped conical breasts and very high pointed shoulders.

In 1981, when *Metal Priestess* was recorded and these photos of Wendy, Wes and Richie were taken for the cover, black leather S&M-referencing clothing items like what Wendy and Wes and Richie are wearing weren't easily available. There were no Hot Topic shops selling mass-produced "punk rock" black leather wear in malls just yet. (The retailer started in 1988.) It would also be quite a few years before fashion designers such as Jean-Paul Gaultier, John Galliano and Alexander McQueen would send leather and studs down Fashion Week runways to be knocked off and mass-produced into the mainstream.

Metal Priestess finds Wendy truly *singing* in a carrying-a-tune manner on the opening track, "Lunacy." The lyrics of this song address the Moon and its power, which fits in with the significance of the pentagram on the cover--witchcraft invokes the power of the moon as well as it uses this symbol. Some lyrics of "Lunacy" are: "Behold the power the full moon/Dichotomy from outer space/dominates the human race."

Wendy invokes a prince of darkness on "Doom Song"which opens with keyboards played by Wes Beech. "Sex Junkie" appears here as well as on Beyond The Valley of 1984 and Wendy sounds like a demanding dominatrix ("You're a sex junkie/you'll do as I please.") The lyrics of "Masterplan", (which also appears on *Beyond The Valley of 1984*), lash out at power abusing members of the patriarchy ("Masterplan/macho man/masterplan/it makes you feel so virile/Masterplan deliveryman masterplan/You'd like to rule the world").

There's an apocalyptic theme to *Metal Priestess,* Most notably on the song "12 Noon" where the lyrics list bad things that will disappear with the end of the world, ranging from neutron bombs and cowboy politics to hydrogenated oil and potato starch.

The *Metal Priestess* EP finds the Plasmatics crossing a bridge from the punk flavor of their previous albums to the heavy metal genre at a time when the punk and metal camps were diametrically opposed to each other. This was a very brave move. Many successful bands just keep giving their fans new albums with the same formula of music. For the Plasmatics to make their sound harder and heavier and dress in the accoutrements of metal probably challenged their fans quite a bit. The lyrics on the inner sleeve are rendered in an Olde English/Germanic font typically associated with heavy metal as well.

The inclusion of "Sex Junkie" and "Masterplan," which were on *Beyond The Valley of 1984*, on *Metal Priestess* would seem to ease Plasmatics fans into the band's new direction, saying that they're not totally disowning all that had come before.

Metal Priestess marked the debut of Chris "Junior" Romanelli as bassist for the Plasmatics. Two drummers are also credited on the EP – namely Joey Reese and Tony Petri. In 1982, T.C. Tolliver answered an ad in *The Village Voice* for a drummer for the Plasmatics. He stood out enough among the many drummers who auditioned and joined the band. As Tolliver stated in a 2008 video interview: "I saw them *[Plasmatics]* on Tom Snyder and I thought, 'Where's the beat? If I was in that band, that band would be hot!" In the same interview, Tolliver also says, "My style of playing made that whole Plasmatics sound.

The Plasmatics' next full-length album, *Coup d'Etat* (the title is the French for "quick takeover of the government by the military") released on Capitol in 1982, was produced by Dieter Dierks, who was renowned for his production work with The Scorpions. Recorded at Dierks's studios near Cologne, The album opens with "Put Your Love In Me" where Wendy's all appetite, demanding sex as she also does on "Rock 'n' Roll." Wendy screams a lot on "Stop." "Country Fairs" finds her surprisingly and sweetly singing the refrain "Country fairs/village squares/Sunday school/ golden rule."

Wendy being Wendy though, don't let that sweetness of her vocals fool you; an apocalyptic scenario unfolds in "Just Like On TV" – an invasion by giant apes, "massive global eruptions" dreams and nightmares manifesting simultaneously.

A Plasmatics release titled *Coup de Grace* (the title meaning a final blow or shot given to kill a wounded person or animal) was a demo recorded in 1981 at Electric Ladyland studio (the New York recording studio initially built and owned by Jimi Hendrix). Dan Hartman and Rod Swenson produced these songs prior to the actual recording of the *Coup d'Etat* album. Regarded as a rehearsal for *Coup d'Etat*, *Coup de Grace* was recorded in just one week and *Coup d'Etat* was recorded in two months. Of the eleven tracks on *Coup de Grace*, only one, "Uniformed Guards," does not appear on *Coup d' Etat* and the song "Mistress of Passion " became "Mistress of Taboo" on *Coup d'Etat*.

The tapes for *Coup de Grace* were thought lost, but once they were discovered, were released as a CD and vinyl album after Wendy's death. Given the circumstances of Wendy's suicide, the title *Coup de Grace* has a certain poignancy.

Coup d'Etat finishes with "The Damned"-- maybe the closest the Plasmatics ever came to having a hit. This video for this song was a favorite of MTV clown princes Beavis and Butt-Head and was often featured on their show. The video for "The Damned," shot in the Mojave Desert, finds Wendy at one point driving a school bus with the door torn off. She drives said bus through a wall of TVs in the desert and the wall explodes.

There is a disclaimer at the beginning of the video for "The Damned" imploring viewers that "you should not attempt this at home" and that the video was created and performed by "professional conceptual artists." In a 1998 *Hartford Courant* article, reporter

Roger Caitlin wrote that in 1993, Beavis and Butt-Head were blamed for encouraging pyromania by watching the video for "The Damned." He states that Beavis yelled "Fire! Fire!" when this video was shown and that supposedly prompted an Ohio 5-year old to burn down his parents' mobile home in which his two-year old sister died.

There were other fire references in the MTV cartoon show, including a scene where one of the characters sets the other's hair on fire with a match and spray from an aerosol can. Three girls, also in Ohio in 1993, started a fire after watching this scene. Soon after these incidents, MTV removed all fire references from *Beavis and Butt-Head*.

Carole Robinson, Senior Vice President of MTV at that time was quoted in an article by Lee Marguiles in *The Los Angeles Times* as saying "Beavis and Butt-head' is made for teen-agers and young adults, who make up the overwhelming majority of its audience," Robinson said. "These viewers see the cartoon for what it is--an exaggerated parody of two teen-age misfits whose antics take place in a cartoon world, antics they know are obviously unacceptable and not to be emulated in real life."

"While we do not believe the 'Beavis and Butt-head' cartoon was responsible," She said, "we feel the steps we are taking are the proper ones."

In "The Damned" video, Wendy is unstoppable. She sprained her ankle during its October 1982 desert shoot and considering the impossibility of doing a reshoot because of the high-stakes, one-take-only stunts, she insisted on continuing the shoot with her ankle wrapped in gaffer's tape.

Wendy looks like the ultimate woman warrior in this video. Her blonde Mohawk stretches skyward. Her body is exceptionally taut – her belly has such little fat that it looks almost concave. She's wearing what looks like a ripped black tee shirt covering her chest and more ripped black fabric around her waist, accented with silver chains. On her elbows are armbands with very long, pointy spikes and she's wearing black boots.

She pulls off stunts perfectly; looking ferocious and scowling and bearing all her teeth as she drives the school bus from the Tombstone

High School District with the driver's side door removed. There is a time bomb in the driver's area of the bus and dark fabric covers the windshields. This must have hampered her vision as she drove, yet Wendy hits her target, crashing the bus into the huge wall of TVs.

Then she's singing on the roof of the school bus as it's moving; falling on her knees and getting up again. We then see Wendy jumping off the school bus roof right before it crashes into another wall of TVs and explodes. She walks away from this fiery spectacle with remarkable nonchalance, personifying the term "badass."

The image of Wendy from "The Damned" video shoot also with her Mohawk and her raised fist became the graphic for an iconic Plasmatics t-shirt that also bears the phrase "The Brainwashed Do Not Know They Are Brainwashed" backwards.

Regarding the recording of *Coup d'Etat* in Germany, Wendy pushed her vocals as far as they could and she reportedly had to get daily treatments in Cologne to prevent damage to her vocal chords.

Dieter Dierks was a strict taskmaster as a producer. When Richie Stotts wasn't playing a certain guitar solo to Dierks' liking, Dierks ordered Stotts to go out to the band's truck and practice it over and over until Dierks was satisfied. Drummer T.C. Tolliver, speaking in *The Wendy O. Williams and the Plasmatics: 10 Years of Revolutionary Rock 'n' Roll* documentary talks about how Dirks could hear a loose screw on Tolliver's snare drum even when the drummer himself couldn't. "We'd play all the songs for *Coup d'Etat* all the way through over and over," Tolliver recalls in the film, "and then Dieter would say 'Ok, we can record now," and I'd think "I thought we *were* recording!"

The cover of *Coup d'Etat*, which featured Wendy sitting atop a tank, straddling its cannon, was photographed in the South Bronx neighborhood of New York City, with abandoned buildings and rubble as background. In the mid-to-late- 1970s, the South Bronx was one of the worst neighborhoods in New York, rife with crime, drugs, and abandoned and burnt out buildings. Circa 1982 (the time of Coup d'Etat's release) things hadn't gotten much better. Around the time of the album cover shoot, President Ronald Reagan gave a speech at the same location promising that the site's urban blight would soon be rebuilt and revived – that didn't happen during his administration. On the cover photo, as Wendy sits atop the tank, Wendy's hair is in a blonde Mohawk and her first is in the air – a gesture of rebellion.

To further the iconoclasm of *Coup d'Etat*, the Plasmatics appropriated backwards masking once again. Conservative pundits back then claimed that there were hidden messages encouraging Satan worship in albums by bands such as Led Zeppelin that could only be heard when the albums were played backwards, hence the term "backwards masking." It all was nothing more than hearsay and a non-phenomenon as it could never be proven.

But the Plasmatics appropriated backwards masking and purposefully included a message on *Coup d'Etat* – one that encouraged listeners to think for themselves. On the vinyl edition of the album, played regularly, the listener would hear a slow, garbled sound, but if they turned it manually in the reverse direction they would hear Wendy saying "consensus programming is dangerous to your health." This was done as a type of parody that was both funny but not funny, tapping into the theater of the absurd that people found somewhat frightening. the Plasmatics did this to address paranoid lunacy, to put out bait for people--which they took, and also to bring people out of their fascistic, moronic closets.

Smiling Wendy with her signature Mohawk.
© MediaPunch Inc/Alamy

Wendy taking over the stage with the Plasmatics.
© MediaPunch Inc/Alamy

Wendy getting close to Plasmatics fans.
© MediaPunch Inc/Alamy

Smash it up: unstoppable Wendy circa 1981.
© MediaPunch Inc/Alamy

Because I'm a woman. I look different. I have a Mohawk. And I'm upset at the status quo.

Unlike New York and Los Angeles, where Plasmatics' iconoclasm and subversion was welcomed and celebrated, The United States Midwest of 1981 was a far more conservative and hostile terrain towards the band.

Wendy had significant run-ins with the police in areas that would come to be known as "flyover states." She (and at times other members of the Plasmatics camp) was arrested in Milwaukee, Cleveland and Chicago. In less than a week Wendy went from being on national television and in the homes of millions of people, getting enthusiastic cheers and applause from the studio audience when the Plasmatics appeared on *Fridays*, to being brought up on criminal charges, suffering physical abuse at the hands of the police and having her mug shot taken with a broken nose, bruises on her face and a cut near her eye.

"A lot of people had never seen a woman with a Mohawk," Maria Raha says in the *Wendy O. Williams 10 Years of Revolutionary Rock and Roll* documentary, in reference to Wendy appearing with the Plasmatics on *Fridays* at this time. "Let alone a woman behaving the way Wendy did on stage. The fright of that probably contributed to a lot of the violence, particularly with the police. I think a lot of men, especially men in small towns were frightened by that."

On January 18, 1981, the Plasmatics were booked to perform at The Palms, a club located at 2616 W. State Street in Milwaukee.

They took the stage in front of a full house at that venue. Chris Foran reported in The *Milwaukee Journal/Sentinel*: "On January 18, 1981, Williams and her punk band, the Plasmatics, performed at the

Palms nightclub. The capacity crowd came to see a performance by an act known for brash music, explosions, Mohawk hairdos, revealing costumes and, well, naughty behavior onstage."

According to *Milwaukee Journal* reviewer Divina Infusino, the show "included Williams making "sexual gestures" and wearing "what appeared to be whipped cream or soap lather (covering) her upper torso."

Undercover police officers were in that crowd, sent there after authorities read a January 16, 1981 article in the "Let's Go" entertainment guide section of the *Milwaukee Sentinel* that said Wendy typically exposed herself onstage during a Plasmatics concert.

After the show, these police officers arrested Wendy and charged her with conduct prohibited in a licensed premises, resisting arrest and battery to police officers - a felony charge.

Wendy stated that she had to walk a gauntlet of police saying things like "Nice knockers. Do you like orgies?" and "Is your band all niggers and queers?" According to Foran's report, about five officers threw Wendy to the ground, choked her and rubbed her face into the icy pavement.

Wendy told the *Milwaukee Journal* that she was held on the ice for a long period of time. An officer pulled up her t-shirt and groped her breasts while she was being put in a police van, she slapped him and a fight broke out. Wendy stated that she was forced to walk from the police van into the police station with no shoes on.

Wendy suffered a broken nose and a wound requiring seven stitches from this incident. "My face is sore, my chest is sore, my arms are sore, I'm sore all over," Wendy told the *Milwaukee Journal*.

According to the article on her arrest in the Jan. 20, 1981 *Milwaukee Sentinel*, "undercover police were sent to the club after authorities read a *Milwaukee Sentinel* article (published in the paper's "Let's Go" section on January 16, 1981) that said Miss Williams exposed portions of her body during her act." And according to the reports of her arrest in the *Journal* and *Sentinel*, police said Williams "kicked one officer, injuring his hand, while Swenson, trying to stop police officers struggling with the singer, kicked another officer in the face."

Rod Swenson tried to intervene and help Wendy and was arrested for obstructing police and battery to police officers -- a felony charge. Swenson himself was beaten by the police officers into semi-consciousness. Wendy and Rod were treated for their injuries in the same hospital and according to the *Wendy O. Williams and the Plasmatics: 10 years of Revolutionary Rock and Roll* documentary, when Wendy asked what happened to Rod she was told he slipped on the ice.

That night, Plasmatics production manager George Pierson made phone call after phone call to agents and lawyers associated with the Plasmatics who might have been able to help release Wendy and Rod from jail. He also ran around Milwaukee trying to find Wendy and Rod who the police were moving from place to place.

"Wendy, Rod, myself and (*pyrotechnics technician*) Pete Cappadocia were all arrested and beat up that night in Milwaukee," says Jean Beauvoir. "Rod changed the story over the years and eliminated our names because we are no longer with the organization. We were all four in *People* magazine for it and we were all booked, beat up and carried to jail in a paddy wagon that night," he says.

According to the *Milwaukee Sentinel*, Wendy and Rod were released on $2000 bail on January 19. They had bruises and cuts on their faces. The date of their trial was set for June 3, 1981.

Photographer Alan Gartzke captured the Milwaukee cops' attack on Wendy on film. Gartzke's photograph of the incident after the Palms appearance shows Wendy screaming while being held down into the ice-covered ground, surrounded by police officers.

According to a January 30, 1981 report in The *Milwaukee Journal,* one of Gartzke's photos showed a police officer "with his hand on Williams' neck, shoving her head into the snow, while she appeared to be crying out in pain." George Pierson, the Plasmatics' production manager says in the *Wendy O. Williams and the Plasmatics 10 years of Revolutionary Rock and Roll* documentary that Gartzke's photograph of Wendy being attacked helped her case.

Chris Foran's look back at the 1981 trial in *The Milwaukee Journal Sentinel* reported that "When the date for Williams and Swenson's trial arrived on June 3, 1981, Assistant District Attorney Peter Kovac first asked a judge to try her and Swenson separately, and then to drop the felony battery charges against both of them." And then, according to the first-day trial story by the *Journal*'s Walter Fee, Kovac suggested Williams might not go to trial at all.

Foran wrote: "Swenson went on trial for his remaining charge, obstructing a police officer. Williams took the stand and, according to a June 6, 1981 story by Walter Fee in The *Milwaukee Journal*, she testified that officers said to her, "We don't like your kind here in Milwaukee…I'll bet you've got a weird sex life."

Wendy later told the San Francisco magazine *Boulevards*: "I was afraid I was dead in Milwaukee. I was afraid they were going to open fire, just start shooting." She told Edouard Dauphin in the September 1981 issue of *Creem* magazine, "When I go into a new town sometimes, I wonder if the police will shoot me."

Maggie Keane, an artist living on New York at the time, had done courtroom sketches in Tucson, where she had graduated from the University of Arizona. She felt an urge to sketch Wendy during her court appearances. As she stated in a 2020 interview: "I was reading about the Plasmatics and their court trials so I called up Stiff Records and said, "Hey I'm a court sketch artist and I'd like to go to these trials and sketch them and Rod Swenson thought that was a great idea, cause he was a Yale art school graduate. The record company was like 'We don't know what to do with these sketches so we kind of don't know where you're coming from,' but then they called back after talking to Rod Swenson about it."

As Keane explained, "There was a lot of time where she was just waiting in the hallway and I was out there too, so I was just sketching her sitting there waiting. And then I put her attorney in there after he did his thing .I remember when she was on the stand being asked about what happened I have a couple of those sketches of her as she's being asked those questions."

When asked about Wendy's demeanor during her court appearances, Keane states: "She was quiet and kind of uncomfortable. It really seemed like if you started a conversation with her about anything else --like kittens or puppies--she would like to talk to you but she was definitely on guard at this trial – at both Milwaukee and Cleveland. "

When sketching Wendy, Keane sought to convey, "just her emotions at retelling the event *[in Milwaukee]*. These cops were just big fat jerks. They didn't even treat her very well in the courtroom. Her attorney was taking care of her, Rod was taking care of her but these cops were just strutting around with this who -do -these –punks-think-they –are kind of attitude."

On April 25, 1981, Wendy was interviewed by *Scranton Times* FOCUS section editor Lance Evans before a Plasmatics performance at the West Side Theater in that Pennsylvania town. She clearly spoke her mind about what had happened to her in the early part of the year and the meaning of what she was doing: "I don't like the kind of vibrations we get when we come into a town like this," she told FOCUS in a private interview, a few hours prior to the.show. "There are many issues that surround the Plasmatics beside the music we play."

"I believe in what we're doing. I really believe in total freedom for the individual. I don't like resistance, I don't like it at all, but it does make me believe that what we're doing is important; that we're getting through to people, even if they don't realize it."

"I really believe that people should think for themselves. I don't think that people are ready to let authorities, police, government, whatever, do all their thinking for them"

"I'm sick and tired of apathy. I'm sick and tired of the violence I see around me. I want to tell people that they just don't have to accept those things, they do have choices, that they can fight the system. Rock 'n' roll is my medium and the Plasmatics are my vehicle to encourage people to find things out for themselves, to experience things on their own level."

Further in the article, Evans continues: "For instance, Mick Jagger of the Rolling Stones has continually punctuated that group's act with a variety of seemingly obscene gestures and words. Yet, he doesn't go to work night after night fearing an obscenity arrest.

Williams sees this situation with a kind of bemused detachment.

"Jagger," she *[Wendy]* explains, "is male and that, simply, means he can get away with more stuff than a woman can. Hey, this society's pretty well screwed up. A guy can go out on stage bare chested and do whatever he wants. A woman doing the same thing gets arrested.

Is that hypocrisy, or what? Besides, I think a big difference between Jagger and me is that he's never been political."

"If women can identify with me – and a lot of them do – that's fine, but I don't see myself as any fiery symbol for womanhood. But it's high time people stopped thinking of a woman's body as being dirty. A woman doesn't have to be barefoot, pregnant and in the kitchen to be valid. Let women have some fun. There are infinite possibilities."

"At least, as far as I know, he hasn't been making political statements with his music. I do and, I admit, as far as a lot of these screwed-up values of our current society are concerned, I'm an anarchist. I think a lot of authority figures realize that and they're afraid of me and the freedom of thought I represent. When they arrest me, it isn't because they want to enforce the law as much as they want to intimidate me and others who might agree with what I'm doing."

Rod Swenson also talked to Evans and said: "In some ways," he said, "this continual banging heads with the law is a real drag, but it shows our message is getting across. A lot of people don't want us to play, but a lot of people do."

"When we were on the 'Fridays' show for ABC," Swenson proudly recalls, "the program got its highest rating ever. A couple weeks ago they re-ran it during 'sweeps' week. Now we're working as much as we want. But we have to because, essentially, we haven't made a lot of money from our first album. We make our money by doing these concerts. And," he says with an engaging smile, "we have to make a lot of money these days; you know how expensive lawyers' fees can be."

"What am I going to tell you?" Williams asks, "that our music's easy listening? Not me! The thing about a Plasmatics' show is its force, the intensity of what the audience experiences. You're not going to leave one of our shows humming a catchy little melody the way you would with a lot of commercially successful bands. But you're also not going to walk out without having something in your head to remember us by. When you see the Plasmatics," Williams says with unwavering certitude, "you don't forget us."

Legal fees had piled up to fight the criminal charges Wendy and Rod had faced. the Plasmatics' Legal Defense Fund was created and three benefit shows were mounted at Bond's International Casino in New York's Times Square starting on February 27, 1981. They would need whatever funds they could drum up as the charges in Milwaukee carried potential prison time. Bond's had a large capacity and devoted fans turned up, waiting in the cold. As video cameras filmed them outside the venue, they held their middle fingers up to the cameras and footage of the fans inside Bond's shows some of them smeared with shaving cream in homage to Wendy.

At the first Bond's show, Wendy entered the stage bursting through a huge curtain with a swastika under a red slash and the phrase "Stop The Gestapo." Onstage at these shows were facsimiles of Milwaukee police cars.

"Using sex to create the law is so stupid, and I'm not the kind of person who walks the middle of the line," Wendy said in a June 11, 1981 *Rolling Stone* interview. "We're not out to pick fights. But then the essence of what we do is shaking up the middle class; I think if you don't do that with your music, you're just adding to the noise pollution."

Chris Foran's, *Milwaukee Journal Sentinel* article stated that on June 10, 1981, a week after the trial began, a jury found Rod Swenson not guilty of obstructing an officer. Circuit Judge Clarence Parrish subsequently dismissed the resisting arrest charge against Wendy. In November 1981, the last charge against Wendy – for simulating a sex act onstage – was dismissed. According to an article in *Billboard*, Wendy was cleared of obscenity charges and charges of resisting arrest and battery to a police officer were dropped.

When the Plasmatics appeared for the first time on the *Tomorrow* show with Tom Snyder in 1981, amid the trouble they had with the Milwaukee Police, Wendy sledgehammered a TV and chain sawed a guitar. During her interview segment with Snyder she decried stereotypes and fascism.

The Milwaukee police and the district attorney were invited to appear on *Tomorrow* to rebut but declined to appear.

In the *Wendy O.Williams and the Plasmatics: 10 Years of Revolutionary Rock and Roll* documentary, Chris Knowles states: "The Sex Pistols came to America and people yawned. Nobody cared about the Sex Pistols, they were a joke. the Plasmatics were not only *not* a joke – they were *frightening*. The furor the Plasmatics caused really hadn't been seen since the Sixties. the Plasmatics were almost a test case, something that was seen as a threat to the status quo."

"What happened was not good," says Richie Stotts about the arrests in Milwaukee. "We did a show and all of a sudden there were riot police in the audience. So it was a provoking kind of thing. We went backstage and the police came downstairs, like a vice squad thing. There were riot police in the audience which was uncalled for. It was a little scary. We all huddled backstage. They came to arrest Wendy for simulated masturbation and indecent exposure. They went out to the parking lot: Wendy, Beauvoir, Peter Capadoccia, Rod. I didn't go with them. That's where they roughed up Wendy, Rod got involved and things got out of control there.

"It distracted from the band," he reflects. "It became what the band was about. It did create publicity for the band but I don't know if that's the kind of publicity you'd want."

Ironically, the Palms nightclub would later become a strip club called Hoops, and as a May 14, 2019 article in the *Milwaukee Record* would report, would later become an "all-ages arts and performance hub" called The New State.

Wendy talked about being brutalized by Milwaukee police during an interview with Jeanne Becker on the Toronto TV show *New Music*. "It's terrifying," she said, "At one instance I thought I was dead and I thought I'd never stand up again--it's terrifying*.*" Then she told Becker, "Any history on me – I've never been one to walk the middle of the road, I've always been extreme. I'm a fanatic." In the interview, Becker asks Wendy about being upset by the way some men have regarded her -- "looking at you from the neck down and not the neck up," Becker posits. "I like people to take me as a whole person, the whole being," Wendy replied. "I'm against chauvinism –

whether its male chauvinism or female chauvinism. A pig is a pig. It's high time that people realize that a woman has a mind of her own and the female body is not dirty."

The Plasmatics were scheduled to perform at the Agora club in Cleveland the following night after the show in Milwaukee in January 1981. Rod Swenson wanted to cancel the rest of the tour given the injuries they had suffered in Milwaukee. the Plasmatics were going to begin a tour of Europe in 14 days and Swenson wanted them to take the time to heal and prepare, but Wendy insisted that the Plasmatics perform in Cleveland. As Wes Beech stated in the *Wendy O. Williams 10 Years of Revolutionary Rock and Roll* documentary: "Wendy, being the trouper that she was, she wanted the show to go on."

On January 20, 1981 just a few days after the incidents in Milwaukee, with Wendy still bruised and in pain from being roughed up by the Milwaukee Police, the Plasmatics performed at the Agora club in Cleveland, Ohio. At the Agora, Wendy passed out before the encore and was taken to a hospital. Shortly in the morning, after she was released from the hospital, Cleveland Police arrested her.

As Wes Beech states in the *Wendy O. Williams and the Plasmatics: 10 Years of Revolutionary Rock and Roll* documentary: "It was a scary time because it was us against them. We were worried in every town we were playing."

According to Yxta Maya Murray's article, *"We Just Looked At Them As Ordinary People Like We Were: The Legal Gaze And Women's Bodies"* published in the *Columbia Journal of Gender And Law*, Wendy was arrested by Cleveland police on charges of obscenity for performing onstage wearing just shaving cream on her breasts which melted and left her breasts exposed and "performing a sadomasochistic dance with a sledgehammer."

The *Sarasota Herald-Tribune* reported on January 24, 1981 that "Cleveland police ...arrested the punk rock singer for allegedly pandering obscenity at a Wednesday night performance at a rock nightclub. She was released on $200 bond."

Wendy was tried on obscenity charges in Cleveland in April of 1981 and was found not guilty. As further explained in Yxta Maya

Murray's *Columbia Journal of Gender and Law* Article, Cleveland prosecutor Patrick Roche showed a film of Wendy performing with the Plasmatics which showed Wendy dancing half nude and the cuts and bruises she'd gotten during her Milwaukee arrest.

The jury did not agree with the prosecution's point of view that what Wendy did constituted obscenity; the five man, three woman jury acquitted Wendy after a short deliberation. Fans protested outside the Cleveland courthouse in support of Wendy. Some sat in in the courtroom and cheered when the not guilty verdict was handed down.

Maggie Keane also sketched Wendy during her court appearance in Cleveland. As she recalls: "In Cleveland, she signed one of the pictures for me. She was looking at the picture and she was wearing a black tank top and she was pointing out that her breasts were very visible under this black tank top like I accentuated them for some reason. I didn't know where she was coming from because that was what she was wearing and that was under her tank top and it was almost sounded like she was being prudish almost. I'm thinking, "look at all these other pictures of you, why are you feeling like I overdid it?" But that's what I draw, I draw what's in front of me. I thought it was really strange and I felt like I'd done something wrong, that I objectified her – but even if I did, what's the big deal? This is Wendy O. Williams of the Plasmatics who kind of puts it in your face on a nightly basis, you know? But I felt like I offended her or insulted her in some way and it was weird. She suddenly seemed very demure after that and I thought, "…have I totally misread this woman?"

"Cleveland I never took seriously at all," Wendy said to rock journalist Edouard Dauphin in the September 1981 issue of *Creem.* "We had two local lawyers defending us who made Abbott and Costello look like wizards. It was a real kangaroo court but the jury had to listen to the rantings and ravings of the prosecution. The new District Attorney there is called – are you ready? Jose Feliciano. It wound up that we didn't even present a defense."

Dauphin asked Wendy: "Did you find it hard to sit there and behave in a court of law?"

Wendy replied: "Who said I behaved? I didn't behave. I caused a ruckus in the courtroom. Cleveland is third in the country in rapes and fifth in murders. The D.A. was afraid of the real criminals so he took a cheap shot at me. Because I'm a woman. I look different. I have a Mohawk. And I'm upset at the Status Quo."

In July of 1981 Wendy was arrested for attacking photographer David Barnes who was taking her picture as she jogged along a Chicago lakefront. According to Yxta Maya Murray's article, Barnes had taken three pictures of Wendy when she tried to grab his camera, straddled his back, punched him and kicked him in his back and head, spat at him and a lifeguard and then tried to throw Barnes's camera into Lake Michigan. Wendy was sentenced to one year of supervision and a $35 fine.

In January of 1982, Wendy, Rod Swenson, Jean Beauvoir and Peter Cappadocia filed a $5.95 million dollar lawsuit against the seven Milwaukee police officers involved in Wendy's arrest. In a UPI report, Wendy is quoted as saying "On January 19, 1981, I was arrested on a spurious charge by the Milwaukee police, taken out to the back of the Palms night club and sexually assaulted and beaten...my shirt was pulled up, my pants pulled down, my breasts and buttocks were squeezed as my face was pushed, again and again, into the icy ground." The article states that Wendy called for the removal of Police Chief Harold A. Brier and the resignation of Milwaukee County District Attorney E. Michael McCann.

"The citizens of Milwaukee must not tolerate a gestapo police force that makes a mockery of law and order," Wendy said.

The case went to trial in Milwaukee Country Circuit Court in the fall of 1984 where Wendy, Swenson, Beauvoir and Cappadocia sued seven officers involved in Wendy's arrest for deprivations of constitutional rights and false arrest. According to Yxta Maya Murray's article, the false arrest claim was dropped during trial and Wendy testified that as a result of the police beating, she suffered from problems hearing and singing and pain in her ears during travel.

According to Murray's interview with former Milwaukee city attorney R. Scott Ritter, two photographs were introduced into the trial: the defense submitted "a picture of Williams onstage covered with whipped cream provocatively touching her groin," Ritter said he used this to dispute the false arrest claim using this photo as visual evidence that the officers would have probable cause to believe Wendy was guilty of obscenity. Murray's article goes on to say that the court ordered the image removed after the false arrest charge was dropped, but the jury did see it. The second image was the Alan Gartzke photograph which the plaintiffs used to support their claim of excessive force and violation of civil rights.

In Murray's article, Ritter goes on to explain why he made many references to Wendy's sexual provocation onstage and in her performing with Captain Kink's Sex Fantasy Theater; according to Murray's article he said he intended it to show that Wendy had not sustained any damages, in the event that sexual assault was found by the jury. "She claims that they made a comment about her body," he said to Murray, "and that caused her huge emotional damages [and we were trying to show that]…she was not this shy girl."

Murrays' article also reports that Wendy testified to sexual assault and verbal abuse by the officers; she said that police officers stood in a circle around her, made lewd remarks about her body, put their hands on her breasts and buttocks and made racist comments about African American men in her band, namely Jean Beauvoir.

The article goes on to say that Jane Peschman, the nurse who treated Wendy at Mount Sinai Hospital in Milwaukee, testified that Wendy had been "scared and hysterical" during treatment and that Wendy thought she had been "manhandled." The defendant's expert witness, Dr. S. Frederick Horwitz testified that Wendy's ears were normal and her throat was in excellent condition.

The jury deliberated for five hours and ruled in favor of the Milwaukee police, ruling that the six officers (a seventh had died after the lawsuit was filed) did not use excessive force and that Williams wasn't unlawfully arrested.

Wendy performed in Milwaukee again a few times after losing the lawsuit. She had stated that she would return to Milwaukee when Police Chief Harold Breier retired. He did so on June 30 of 1984 and Wendy performed again in Milwaukee a month before the beginning of the civil trial in the fall of 1984.

Later on, according to the *Wendy O. Williams and the Plasmatics: 10 Years of Revolutionary Rock and Roll* documentary, a lawsuit was also filed against Wendy by a young man in Madison, Wisconsin who jumped onstage during a Plasmatics performance and tried to put his hand between Wendy's legs. Wendy hit him on the head with a microphone and he sued for excessive damages.

Legal bills for Wendy and Swenson piled up; it was very expensive, during the civil suit trial in Milwaukee, to fly out expert witnesses, pay for their lodging, etc. Also, the stigma of being arrested and/or being brought up on charges and suing the Milwaukee police officers —regardless of whether Wendy and Ron won or lost in court—greatly besmirched the perception of Wendy and the Plasmatics. Conservative groups put pressure on promoters to cancel Plasmatics performances and tried to stop them from coming to their towns.

A review of the Plasmatics in *Creem* by Cyril Blight, at around the time of Wendy's arrests, attacked the sexism of those who "can't handle … even resent the very idea of a woman singing rock 'n' roll with ferocity -- which is to say the same qualities they would applaud if they were coming from a man, providing there was a man around today with the balls to do that."

The End of the Plasmatics

By the early-to-mid-eighties, the legal wrangling was taking its toll on the Plasmatics. Aside from the fees they had to contend with from the Milwaukee and Cleveland incidents, more and more promoters across the U.S. didn't want to book them, citing fear that a Plasmatics gig would result in a clash with local law enforcement and bad results for everyone involved. In the *Wendy O. Williams and the Plasmatics: 10 Years of Revolutionary Rock and Roll* documentary, Rod Swenson is quoted as saying: "Promoters would say they loved Wendy but were afraid of local authorities. Conservative groups would complain as soon as shows were announced."

Lance C. Phillips was sound engineer for the Plasmatics on the *Coup d'Etat* tour. He had been working for a sound company out of Chicago called DB Sound and had previously done sound for artists such as Joan Jett and Prince on the tour for his *1999* album. As Phillips put it in a 2020 interview: "Plasmatics were not in my wheelhouse as far as my musical taste was concerned, but in the summer of 1983, one of my contacts in the music business got in touch with me and told me they were looking for a sound engineer. The way you get gigs in the music industry, at least back in the '80s it was strictly who you know and everybody refers jobs to other people .It was completely informal. So I thought, 'well, that would be interesting,' and I was available.

"So the first gig I did with them – this is when they were Plasmatics not W.O.W. - it was someplace in Connecticut, and I got there and scoped the place out. I met Rod Swenson and he kind of looked me over and I was told by Jim Cherry who was their stage manager and longtime do-everything -guy, that "Rod's gonna check you out," so I said, "ok." One of the first things he said to me was "Are you familiar with our latest album, the newest album? "and I said "Yeah, I've listened to it, I'm familiar with the songs. That was *Coup de Etat*. And one of the first things he asked me was, "What exactly is a coup d'etat?" and I said "That's the forceful overthrow of a government by the military,' "so that was like "Check!" and from that point on I was good to go."

Rod, Wendy and the band liked the way Phillips mixed Wendy's vocals. They had been having problems finding a sound engineer who could produce the blend of impact and volume they wanted while keeping vocals at the forefront of the mix. As Phillips said, "I had no problem with that and that was the kind of first thing that endeared me to them."

Phillips was somewhat surprised when he met Wendy. "She wasn't anything like I'd expected, " he says "My first meeting with her was for sound check and here's this medium height blonde comes running in dressed in khaki shorts, sweat-socks, sneakers, a tee shirt, hair pulled back in a ponytail - she looked like a coed. And I thought, "*this* is Wendy?" I quickly learned that there was quite a difference between the perception of Wendy and the reality of Wendy.

"The perception was that she was probably this crazy half-woman half-animal, ready for anything druggie. But the reality was she was very quiet, very contemplative, very nice and very pleasant. There was a complete disconnect between what happened when she was onstage and what happened when she was offstage. It was kind of a metamorphosis. When she was onstage, man—don't fuck with her.

There was any number of times during the shows where she was very audience interactive and guys would get too handsy and at least twice she cold cocked guys with the wireless microphone and broke the microphone."

Creative strife as well was casting a pall over the band. Capitol Records didn't know what to do with a band who had no interest in making "radio friendly" music that would go along to get along with the status quo when the very essence of the Plasmatics was undermining the status quo. Capitol discontinued their relationship with the Plasmatics after *Coup d'Etat*.

In the Eighties, before the do-it-yourself indie groundswell would happen ten years later, rock bands needed the backing of a major record company paired with a network of local promoters who would facilitate concerts they could play to promote their records. That's how bands earned their keep and had thriving careers. But the Plasmatics' blend of provocation and chaos was making it exponentially difficult for the Plasmatics to be the Plasmatics. As stated in the *Wendy O. Williams and the Plasmatics*: *10 Years of Revolutionary Rock and Roll* documentary, with no record company and fewer and fewer concert opportunities, Wendy and Rod felt that a point when diminishing returns meant having to compromise the integrity of the effort they'd shut down.

Lance C. Phillips did sound for the last Plasmatics concert. "It was at a small club in, I believe, New Jersey, and it was no sound no fury and signified nothing," he said. "They just petered out. This was the way the Plasmatics ended; not with a bang but a whimper. I don't know if they said anything like "Come see Plasmatics last show!" I don't even know if we all realized it or it was common knowledge, I think it was because I know towards the end there was a lot of antagonism between Richie Stotts and Rod, which is why when they reformed Richie was on the outs and Wes Beech was a carryover from the Plasmatic era as was T.C. Tolliver and there was a new guitarist and bass player and they were much more of a straight forward heavy metal-oriented four piece with Wendy as the frontwoman."

Jean Beauvoir had already left the Plasmatics before they recorded *Coup d'Etat*. Chris Romanelli took over from him on bass. "The band was heading in a direction where they were going to lose what made them unique," reflects Beauvoir. "Everyone in the band was an individual –Wendy, of course, Richie who was 6'8" and kind of transvestite looking—to me that was the secret sauce. I didn't like that they were going to be more standard metal. "

When asked about the end of the Plasmatics, Richie Stotts clearly states that the band was very dear to him. "How did the band end? Well that's a bone of contention and I get myself into trouble talking about it every freakin' time. I was with the band right from the beginning. I put my heart and soul, everything into that band. I didn't know anything, I was from upstate New York, I liked The Grateful Dead and David Bowie, I was all mixed up and I came down here...that band meant everything to me. I was very loyal and I worked hard and I loved it. We had some of the best fans. Our fans are the coolest fans because we had such a cross-spectrum of people. We had some famous musicians and artists who loved the band – but also our regular fans were really great. I'm still in touch with a bunch. You should see the letters I get – 'you changed my life…your guitar playing…The Plasmatics, Wendy.' There's a really great bunch of people out there," he says emphatically.

"I always wanted to have a solo career, " says Jean Beauvoir "and it was David Lee Roth who came to one of our shows in, I think, Pasadena and we went out that night and also the money wasn't right and they wanted me to sign a new contract and I didn't want to do that so I ended up leaving."

"I did a lot after that," Beauvoir continues "I joined Little Steven's band, I had an offer from Prince, which I didn't take. I did a solo record which wound up going platinum and I had a song on the soundtrack to *Cobra*, the Sylvester Stallone film. Then I wrote songs with KISS and The Ramones, I did solo records, I've worked quite a bit. Right now I've been working with Lita Ford and a band called Lordi from Europe who dress as monsters, I produced a song for N'SYNC, I've worked with Lionel Richie, Debbie Harry. I just continue to work."

"Jean wasn't in the band anymore, Chris Romanelli joined the band, we had a different drummer. We made the transition from punk to metal," says Richie. "That transition from *New Hope For the Wretched*, when we started listening to Judas Priest, when Chris Romanelli joined the band --he was more metal like Black Sabbath, when we were with Capitol records they wanted to get a producer by that time we worked with Dan Hartman. I started listening to all these bands I used to hate like Journey, AC/DC, well I didn't hate them…I wasn't listening anymore to The Buzzcocks but I was like 'Wow , I can see the whole big thing,' so I think I and everyone including Rod and Wendy wanted to be bigger, we wanted to be better and we just didn't want to keep playing *New Hope For The Wretched*, we wanted to change with every album and from that certain things were lost, some of the humor. I think *Coup d'Etat* is a really good metal album. It was produced by Dieter Dirks. So how the band ended was after we did *Coup d'Etat* for Capitol, we made mistakes. We had the opportunity to be on *Saturday Night Live* and it didn't happen. Management didn't want us to do that.

"That's what I think," Richie continues, "Judas Priest and Ozzy wanted to open for us. Then we ended up opening for KISS. I regret not being on *Saturday Night Live*. We had an opportunity. We had an opportunity to be in the movie *Cruising*—no."

(Cruising is a 1980 film directed by William Friedkin--famous for directing *The French Connection* and *The Exorcist*--starring Al Pacino, Paul Sorvino and Karen Allen. Pacino plays a NYPD undercover cop investigating a string of murders in the Meatpacking District's gay club scene. Rod and Wendy didn't want to participate in the film because they thought it would negatively stereotype gays. Some members of the New York gay community protested the filming. Seminal L.A. punk band The Germs were then tapped to record music for the film but only one song of theirs, "Lion's Share," was used in the soundtrack. When *Cruising* was released it was given an X rating, got poor reviews and fared badly at the box office.)

"My feeling was…these were mistakes," Richie continues, "I was a young kid – Rod was the experienced person, he was making the decisions. But did I feel bad that we didn't take those opportunities – yes. Now that might be a bone of contention but I'm just telling the truth."

As Jack Mulholland puts it, "Certain bands…the front man and the guitarist are the face of the band. The Who were able to carry on after the death of Keith Moon and John Entwhistle because Roger Daltrey and their genius guitar player…because you had Pete Townshend, brilliant guitarist up front, you can still legitimately call them The Who. As long as Keith Richards and Mick Jagger are alive you can call them the Stones. But if you take Richie away from the Plasmatics and you just have Wendy up front, there's no one else who can compete – it's not the same band without Richie."

The W.O.W. Factor

After the release of *Coup d'Etat*, Capitol Records did not have strong feelings about working with the Plasmatics, perhaps being more interested in bands on their label who had more typically commercial potential such as Duran Duran and The Motels. In light of this, the Plasmatics started to disintegrate. As Richie Stotts puts it: "What happened was, we went on tour with KISS as the opening act and I don't think Capitol records wanted to continue their relationship with Wendy and the Plasmatics. Ya gotta talk to Capitol. The band I think was winding to an end. Gene Simmons came to some of our rehearsals. We were working on new songs for another record. I worked on some songs with him, my name is on what became the Wendy O. Williams album.

"Gene told me that Plasmatics did not have a good connotation with the name and if Wendy started fresh she could be the next Joan Jett. But they wanted to go a different way where I didn't fit in any more. It broke my heart," says Richie. "You can spin it any way you want. But that's the story, Gene Simmons got involved, they did put out that album, Wendy O. Williams produced by Gene Simmons. Then I wasn't in touch for a long time with those guys."

At the Pine Bluff Arkansas opening of the 1983 10th Anniversary US KISS Creatures of the Night tour with Plasmatics as opening act, local church officials held a "record breaking party" where they smashed up "demonic" records before KISS and Plasmatics played live at the Pine Bluff convention center. *Entertainment Tonight* interviewed a pastor of a local church about the religious protesting. Onstage that night, Wendy's legs were bare save for black leather boots, black knee coverings with long metal spikes and matching elbow pads with similar spikes and she's wearing black tape on her nipples. Her hair is in a blonde Mohawk with the sides Wendy's natural brown. At the concert she demolished a TV and held its carcass high above her head. She also cut apart a black electric guitar.

"We really blew Gene away when we did that KISS tour." TC Tolliver said in a 2008 video interview.

The set list for Plasmatics' Detroit show at the Cobo Arena on this tour contained several songs from *Coup d' Etat* and a medley of "Living Dead", "Masterplan" and "Tight Black Pants" from *New Hope For The Wretched* and *Beyond The Valley of 1984*. Their set clocked in at 36 minutes and 34 seconds.

Because she was always the focal point of the Plasmatics, it's not entirely surprising that Wendy would go solo. She had dipped her toe in the pool of non- Plasmatics waters in 1982 when she recorded a cover of Tammy Wynette's signature song "Stand By Your Man" as a duet with Lemmy Kilmister, lead singer and bassist of Motörhead. Recorded at Eastern Sound Studios in Toronto, the resulting EP consists of "Stand By Your Man," Wendy singing Motörhead's "No Class" and Lemmy singing Plasmatics' "Masterplan."

Backing them is a hybrid of Plasmatics and the English hard rock band: Wes Beech on rhythm guitar, Lemmy duetting with Wendy on vocals and playing bass, Richie Stotts on lead guitar and Phil Taylor from Motörhead on drums.

Lemmy, in his autobiography *White Line Fever*, co-authored with Janiss Garza writes: "After [Motörhead's] EP with Girlschool hit, People were always on us to collaborate on records, especially with girls. And I really enjoy making records with birds. Eight geezers in the studio can really be a drag—recording with girls usually produces better results, because it causes an interesting kind of friction, and also the scenery is a bit better! Abrasiveness and scenery – I'm all for both, and it was clear I'd get that from Wendy O. It was touted as this extraordinary combination of punk and heavy metal – two warring factions at the time. "

Motörhead guitarist Eddie Clarke was supposed to produce those tracks. To Lemmy's dismay, Will Reid Dick (a British rock producer who Lemmy referred to as Evil Red Dick) was present. "The session was problematic to say the least," Lemmy says in the book, "Wendy took a long time to get in tune, and it wound Eddie up. She tried her parts a few times and she sounded terrible, I will say that, you think she was never going to get it, but I knew she would if I just worked with her."

Lemmy goes on to say that matters were made worse by Eddie not playing guitar and solely working as producer. "We were using Wendy's guitarist from the Plasmatics, with me and Phil on bass and drums." Ultimately Eddie was so unhappy with The Who scenario that he quit Motörhead during this recording session. As Lemmy reflects, "Actually, Eddie used to leave the band about every two months, but this time it just happened that we didn't ask him back."

In Tammy Wynette's recording of "Stand By Your Man," the country doyenne sings as if she's choking back tears. That may have to do with Wynette being married five times -- just what did standing by these men do for her?

Wendy did manage to get her vocals together. In her version of Wynette's song Wendy sounds cantankerous and abrasive, almost daring the listener to give up her freedom and acquiesce to her man— but look out, she'll be sorry. "Country music is symbolic of conservative lunacy," Wendy said to Sandy Robertson in the September 18, 1982 issue of the British music magazine *Sounds*, adding: "The idea of doing a raunchy, rock version of the song immediately appealed to me…I like Motörhead because to me they seem like a band to which nothing is sacred. I like Lemmy's voice, it's the male version of mine."

Released on the English record label Bronze (home to Motörhead), the photos on the *Stand By Your Man* EP, taken by Rod Swenson under the name Butch Star, show Wendy and Lemmy standing in a graffiti-covered New York City subway car – a long way away from Nashville. Under her leather jacket, Wendy is just wearing pasties on her nipples. Lemmy has his arm resting on her shoulder. There has been some speculation that Lemmy and Wendy had some sort of romantic connection but reportedly Wendy regarded him with repulsion. In this cover photo for the EP, Wendy is looking askance at Lemmy, as if she wants him to go away.

In 1984, Wendy recorded her first solo album, *W.O.W.* The album finds Wendy singing hard-driving assertive anthems—songs with titles like "I Love Sex (And Rock 'n' Roll)," "It's My Life,"—which was the single off the album and appeared on the soundtrack to the film *Reform School Girls* that Wendy appeared in—and "Bump And Grind," "Ready To Rock," "Priestess," and "Ain't None of Your Business."

With the Plasmatics having opened for KISS on their Creatures of the Night tour, and Wendy being willing to embark on a solo career, Gene Simmons produced Wendy's solo debut as well as playing bass on it. It was released on the Passport label. Wendy's transition from fronting the Plasmatics to having her own band with W.O.W. wasn't a total dismissal of her previous group – Wes Beech and T.C. Tolliver play on the album and Richie Stotts, Chris Romanelli and Rod Swenson are credited with writing some of the songs.

Writing and performing credits are split between members of the Plasmatics (and Rod Swenson) and KISS on the W.O.W. album. Gene Simmons credits himself on W.O.W. as Reginald Van Helsing, a nod to Abraham Van Helsing, a character from Bram Stoker's *Dracula*. Simmons plays bass on the album and his production gives the songs on *W.O.W.* a certain heavy sheen. He co-wrote the opening track, "I Love Sex (and Rock 'n' Roll) with Wes Beech, Rod Swenson, T.C. Tolliver and Richie Stotts and co-wrote "It's My Life" with KISS cohort Paul Stanley. Simmons along with their KISS members Eric Carr and Vinnie Vincent wrote "Ain't None of Your Business." From the Plasmatics camp, Wes Beech, Rod Swenson, Chris Romanelli and Stotts wrote "Priestess." Swenson and Romanelli wrote "Opus in Cm7" and they, along with Richie Stotts wrote "Ready to Rock." Beech, Swenson, Romanelli, Tolliver and Stotts wrote "Bump and Grind." Simmons and Mitch Weissman wrote "Thief In The Night." Adam Mitchell, who had co-written songs with KISS in addition to writing songs recorded by Olivia Newton-John, Johnny Cash and Nicolette Larson, co-wrote "Legends Never Die" with Simmons and Micki Free, guitarist for the group Shalamar."

Backing Wendy's vocals up instrumentally on the *W.O.W.* album are Michael Ray on lead guitar (who had recorded some lead guitar parts for KISS's *Creatures of the Night* album), Wes Beech on rhythm guitar, Simmons on bass and T.C. Tolliver on drums, again seeming to make a transition from Wendy's days in the Plasmatics to a solo debut album squired by KISS.

Mitch Weissman co-wrote the song "Thief In The Night" with Gene Simmons that's on the *W.O.W.* album and he played piano on the *W.O.W.* album track "Opus in c Minor 7th" on *W.O.W.* He describes meeting Wendy while the album was being recorded:

"Gene and I went out to New Jersey where they were recording the album and she came into the control room after we got there. She was very sweet, coming out in her onesie pajamas, with bunny slippers. The first thing she said to me was "Wow, those lyrics are kind of demonic!" We all started laughing! She was very cool to hang with. I had come out to watch Michael Ray record his guitar solo over that song and to sing on several other ones. I also played the piano on "Opus in c minor 7th."

Weissman discusses the songwriting process with Simmons:

"I had the music pretty much done for the entire song which I had presented to Gene for lyric and melody ideas. It was to be for KISS primarily but the Wendy project was just perfect for it. Gene and I would write in a very loose kind of style. Say anything. Let it hit the wall and see what stuck! That's about the best way to put it!"

"Her vocal tracking was pretty much done by the time I got out there," Weissman recalls, "I believe she'd already sang "Thief in The Night." Most of the tracks were already in the can. We just came in to overdub and add parts. Me, Gene and Eric Carr on that one day in particular. Writing with Gene was always pretty easy. If I remember correctly "Thief in The Night" was just a song we were working on for general purposes. KISS recorded it years later after Wendy recorded it first."

Given Simmons's production, plus the songwriting and playing by pretty much all the members of KISS, makes *W.O.W.* sound quite a bit like a 1984 KISS record with Wendy on vocals. Yet the *W.O.W.* album may have perplexed Plasmatics fans. It had its share of supporters and detractors.

Kerrang! , the British hard rock magazine, was very supportive of Wendy. Malcolm Dome, an editor at the magazine, named *W.O.W.* as his choice for album of the year in 1984.

Ralph Heibutzki, writing in AllMusic.com stated: "In some ways, Williams' first solo venture amounts to a watered-down echo of the Plasmatics' own bid for mainstream success, *Coup d'Etat* (1982), minus the latter record's radical political bent. That's not surprising, with the ever-career-conscious Simmons manning the producer's chair. Despite his best efforts, however, Williams would stay a quintessential cult artist. While not a remarkable record, WOW offers a convincing enough glimpse of the stardom that should have been hers all along."

As James Greene, Jr. wrote in the Hard Noise section of The Hard Times.net. website, regarding the presence of KISS and Plasmatics members on the *W.O.W.* album:

"In fact, the members of Wendy's "former" group take up all the instrument slots and writing credits not attributed to KISS. *WOW* was released via the Passport record label; it's been speculated that the Plasmatics name was only dropped to sidestep a potential legal quagmire with the group's original label, Capitol Records. So this is a triple threat: a Wendy O. Williams solo debut, a lost Plasmatics album, and a secret Kiss album. *WOW's* also got Micki Free on acoustic guitar, which might technically make it a Shalamar side project. The mainstream press never took KISS seriously, so they barely had any truck for Wendy O. Williams. *WOW's* release was treated as a perverse, outrageous curiosity (just like everything else Williams did with the Plasmatics). One of the kinder statements came from Terry Atkinson in the *Los Angeles Times*, who that October likened Williams's searing voice to "a cross between Joan Jett and a real jet."

The W.O.W. album is fairly removed from Wendy's destructive, outwardly directed Plasmatics days; here she revels in songs about herself; what she wants and how she'll get it.

On the W.O.W. album, Wendy is exuberant in her sense of pleasure and seems to be making her declaration of independence, not caring what people think of her, not wanting to be told what to do as she roars and wails. She breaks away from these themes on the slower yet still heavy songs "Legends Never Die" and "Opus in Cm7."

The video for "It's My Life," seems to follow-up from where the video of "The Damned," left off with some extra images: The video starts with Wendy shaking hands with a crowd of adoring fans as she sings. Then she engages in a wrestling bout with a brunette female wrestler and argues with the referee, shoving him away at one point.

In footage shot in the desert, Wendy is driving an orange convertible with the W.O.W. logo painted on the door as she sings the song's lyrics about self-determination. She looks at the camera and holds up her middle finger. We see video images of a bulldozer destroying a typical suburban home—later we see Wendy in the bulldozer's driver's seat - perhaps making a comment on how Wendy adamantly refused to be middle class.

Then a biplane hovers over the convertible and a rope ladder drops down over it. As the car is running, Wendy gets out of the driver's seat and starts climbing the rope ladder up to safety. The car falls over a cliff.

Approximately six years later, the film *Thelma and Louise* would be celebrated as a testament to female empowerment, but (spoiler alert) at the end of the film, Thelma and Louise stay in their convertible as it goes over a cliff plunging them to a fiery death.

The sight of women committing suicide isn't empowering. Rather seeing a woman escape danger is.

Granted, Wendy was rescued by the plane with the rope ladder hovering above her – and Thelma and Louise weren't so lucky. Perhaps the video for "It's My Life" is more empowering because Wendy escapes from certain death and *lives* as the car goes over the desert cliff.

It's especially poignant that despite Wendy successfully pulling off such dangerous stunts in her videos, she committed suicide some years later.

Later on, as the controversy over labeling music with explicit content bubbled up in the news, Wendy spoke out against this form of censorship. In 1985, wearing a t-shirt bearing the phrase Eat Your Honey, Wendy appeared on a panel put together in New York by the National Academy of Recording Arts and Sciences (aka NARAS, the organization behind the Grammys) to discuss the issue of labeling records for explicit content. Also on the panel were Senator Paula Hawkins, founding member of the Parents' Music Resource Council, recording artist Mtume, Barry Mayo, General Manager of New York radio station WRKS and attorney Alan H. Levine. Record producer Bob Porter moderated.

According to a report in the September 25, 1985 issue of *Billboard*, Mayo opened the discussion by saying he was "violently opposed to a rating system," saying it would "affect artists' creativity."

Wendy stated that "Some product put out is offensive and sexist," but argued that there are more things in the world that are more offensive such as government spending, the arms race and television. Wendy also noted that the PMRC was looking at material released over the last few years. "That's [approximately] 50,000 songs," Wendy said, "judging from the handful they have come up with there is not a problem at all."

In her book, *Raising PG Kids in an X-Rated Society* (published by Abingdon Press 1987), Senator Paula Hawkins wrote:

"I suggested to the panel that parents have a right to know what their children are buying and hearing. Wendy O. Williams, a Grammy nominee, replied that I was upset about these songs simply because I can't handle the possibility that my own child might masturbate....Ms. Williams obviously considered me a neurotic Washington housewife who dislikes sex. She proceeded to read from the Song of Solomon and *Twelfth Night*. It almost seemed worth the pain to hear a woman who sings songs like "(Work That Muscle) F*** That Booty" recite the Bible and Shakespeare."

At a congressional hearing, Senator Paula Hawkins waved Wendy's first solo album, *W.O.W,* in front of the Congressional committee regarding censorship of music. In this instance, Wendy was described as an abnormal, oversexed woman who was a threat to young people.

Yet the songs on the *W.O.W.* album are not inciting to listener to do anything dangerous to themselves nor others. All the songs come from Wendy's point of view and seem to be about her feelings and ideas. Listening to the *W.O.W.* album, one doesn't feel threatened or offended; when Wendy sings "I Love Sex (and Rock 'n' Roll)" she's articulating feelings that many people have – it's a safe bet that a large amount of people all over the world love sex and rock 'n' roll too.

If Tipper Gore was afraid of her children being curious about their sexuality because they heard Wendy singing about how much *she* likes sex, chances are they would eventually discover sex on their own, like scores of people before them and since.

The TippWashington wives of the Parents Music Resource Council did get what they wanted, at least to an extent, when the Recording Industry Association of America began labeling music containing explicit content with Parental Advisory stickers circa the mid-to-late eighties. Artists expressed chagrin about these labels. Musicians such as Frank Zappa and Twisted Sister frontman Dee Snider testified at congressional hearings against music censorship. In 1990, to promote their major-label debut album *Goo*, the members of Sonic Youth issued a limited –edition 12-inch record of their single "Kool Thing" with a cartoon saying "Smash The PMRC."

But the way young people purchased music radically changed over the coming years - the days of mothers and children going together to a record store (and even less so, to the record section of a department store) and the child being told mom won't buy them an album bearing the Parental Advisory sticker were fading fast. Via downloading and streaming, young people had direct access to music and concerned parents had to find other ways to monitor how their children were exposed to music that they might find offensive.

Lance C. Phillips, who had been sound engineer for the last Plasmatics tour in 1983 also was sound engineer on Wendy's tour for the *W.O.W.* album.

"The final gig with the Plasmatics was in the summer of '83 and then early 1984 was the beginning of *W.O.W.* and I did a national tour with them that was very informal. It was very low budget. We were traveling in a van, pretty much booking from one gig to another. This was strictly a US tour—East coast, Midwest."

During the Midwest leg of the tour, Phillips had what he regards as a "rather memorable encounter" with a club owner in Kansas:

"We had played a show in Chicago at a club on a Sunday evening and the next show was in Wichita, Kansas on a Tuesday evening. It was a haul but it was definitely doable. When you're traveling on a tour you just put your head down and you drive 24-7 to get to the next gig, You do what you need to do and you just get there.

"Shortly after we got underway on Monday morning the equipment van broke down. This being the age before cell phones, communication was very much an issue; getting in touch with some place to get another van and to get it to the site of where the truck had broken down…it became pretty obvious in a matter of hours that we weren't going to make it to the Wichita show. So Rod and Jim Cherry decided that I would fly to Wichita and advance the show; I would tell the promoter what we needed supplied for band gear on stage and they were going to supply it. There didn't seem to be an issue.

"So I got to Wichita on Tuesday afternoon, got to the venue and it was this big club that was obviously not dealing with anything of the type of music or clientele that would be Wendy O.Williams. It was pretty much a country music place. I thought 'Wow, this is going to be weird, this is not our demographic at all.'

"I went in and found the promoter. He was like a hayseed. I go out and look at the stage and there's the kind of equipment that a band playing at a Holiday Inn lounge would have – little bitty amplifiers, little bitty drum kit – nothing like what I advanced and nothing like I would encounter based on what the promoter had agreed to provide. I had got the impression that when I got off the phone with him that they were like: "Yeah, fuck this guy, they'll be fine."

I was just like, "Wait this isn't going to work. "

"So I got on the phone and when they got into any town Wendy and Rod would check in under an alias at the hotel and Cherry, the stage manager always knows the name that they're registered under and how to get into touch with them. The only saving grace I had in this situation was, one of the first things he told me when the crew and the band arrived was what the contact name was to get in touch with him. I don't know why he did that, he had never done that before. Just some sort of anticipation of something.

Rod and Wendy arrived and Rod asked me, "What's going on? What's the situation?" And I said, "Rod, it's totally inadequate.

There's no way we can do a show here. We should just bail out under the premise that there were conditions agreed upon and they did not meet them and they were pretty much in breach of oral contract. There was nothing on paper but there were conversations. And they said "Well, ok."

"I conveyed this information to Rod and Wendy. Rod and Wendy turned around and started walking out to their limo and the crew started walking to their van. I was lagging behind. Rod and Wendy thought I had gone with the crew in the van and the crew thought I had gone with Rod and Wendy and I got about ten feet out of the club and all of a sudden I found myself in a headlock. Some big gorilla type guy threw me against a wall and put me in a sleeper hold and I was about to lose consciousness. They took me to a little room, a little anteroom next to the stage, like a production office and the bottom line was apparently the club owner was the producer and promoter and he had essentially put everything he had on this concert and if this concert didn't go on he was going to be out of business."

"So, bottom line was, this guy pulled out a little revolver, stuck it to my head and said, 'You get that blonde bitch on the phone, tell her get back here or you're outta here."

"I thought, 'Ok this is serious," so it's about five in the afternoon and I'm like 'Ok, I know how to get in touch with them, thank god.' So I get in touch with Rod and it was one of those conversations where my side of the conversation was "Uh Rod, we need to talk about..." and Rod is on the other side and he says, "Ok Lance, are you in danger?" and I said, "Yeah Rod it's not too good here, I think so," and Rod says, "Are you being held against your will?" "More or less, Rod" So I'm conveying the information to him and he's like, "Ok, don't worry we're going to take care of it." So I get off the phone and I say "It's ok, we're going to be all right." And within about 45 minutes all of a sudden we hear the police from outside saying over a megaphone: "To the people in the club—bring Lance Phillips out!" For once Wendy kind of had the police working *for* her and not against her. This was not that long after Milwaukee. As soon as the police came the people from the club were like, "Oh yeah, there's no problem, he could've gone anytime he wanted to."

"The police, being aware of what they were dealing with in terms of Wendy were doing what they needed to do but they weren't exactly proactive in terms of prosecuting this club owner or what not. It was kind of like "ok we got your guy out, what else do you want us to do?"

"We actually ended up having to do the show. It was a total half-assed disaster of a show. The crowd wasn't that big but at least we were able to get out of dodge. I was quite shaken up, having been roughed up and thrown around. When you have a gun to your head there's a certain degree of clarity that comes along with that. You're very hyper focused on the moment."

Now a solo artist, Wendy's representation in the media was quite varied.

An ardent vegetarian, Wendy was on the cover of *Vegetarian Times* in July of 1984. In her cover photo she has a very sweet, wholesome expression on her face, wearing just some eyeliner and no lip color, her hair pulled back in a ponytail with bangs. The cover line for her story reads: "Raw Food, Raw Talent – The Story Behind Wendy O, Williams" and features a recipe created by Wendy, for a salad dressing. The main ingredient is rejuvelac (wheat berries soaked in water for three days) whirred in a blender with garlic, miso (or soy) sauce, lecithin, cumin, basil, oregano and "fresh herbs of your choice." It has also been reported that Wendy taught a vegetarian cooking class at The Learning Annex in New York City in the early 1990s.

In August of 1984, Wendy was also the first female artist to appear on the cover of *Kerrang!*, the British hard rock/heavy metal magazine. This cover coincided with the release of *W.O.W.* In marked contrast to her fresh-faced smile on the cover of *Vegetarian Times*, her *Kerrang!* cover shows her looking fiercely stern with football player's black under her narrowed eyes. She has a black bullwhip wound around her shoulders and her tattoo of the W.O.W. logo is on her upper arm. (As previously stated, Malcolm Dome, an editor at *Kerrang!* named Wendy's solo *W.O.W.* album as his pick for album of the year).

Wendy was nominated for a Grammy Award in 1985 for Best Female Rock Vocal Performance for the *W.O.W.* album. Did she care? No, not really. Rod Swenson and Wendy were in St. Louis, during Wendy's time portraying Magenta in *The Rocky Horror Show* at the Westport Playhouse when they were contacted about the Grammy nomination. They thought it was a prank at first. Then Wendy and Rod saw reports on TV about the nominations that mentioned Wendy and they realized it was really happening.

But they didn't think Wendy would win, given the record company wrangling and the music-industry popularity contest aspects of the Grammy Awards. Wendy and Rod had no real interest in attending the awards ceremony and weren't the least bit shocked when the gold gramophone statuette went to Tina Turner.

In 1985, David White saw Wendy in this St. Louis production of *The Rocky Horror Show* – a restaging of the musical that came before the quintessential cult film. "Wendy played Magenta," White recalls "Every line delivery was that Wendy O.Williams voice. I remember her coming out into the audience a lot. It was really threatening in a good way. How odd that that was part of her career."

Wendy acted in the film, *Reform School Girls* in 1986, playing Charlie Chambliss, the queen bee bitchy ringleader with lesbian undertones in the girls' dorm at Pridemore Reformatory. As Charlie, Wendy wears pretty much the same attire as she did onstage with W.O.W. – black leather bra, and black leather pants or bikini bottoms. Part campy B-movie, part teen exploitation film, the movie's advertising tagline was So Young, So Bad, So What.

As the opening credits roll, Starring Wendy O. Williams is the first acting credit to appear on screen.

Reform School Girls tells the story of Jenny, played by actress Linda Carol, who gets sent to Pridemore Reformatory after a robbery attempt as a boy's accomplice goes awry. On her first day there, Charlie makes eyes at Jenny over the cafeteria table all the girls are sitting at then has a knockdown drag out fight with the new girl. Later in the film, another new girl—the painfully shy Lisa—is initiated by Charlie and her gang as they brand her on the butt cheek with a hot metal circle while Charlie kisses her. "When we're done with you, you won't even think about guys anymore," Charlie sneers.

"She was the most professional on the set but she was extremely aloof," says Howard Wexler, cinematographer on *Reform School Girls*. "She had her own trailer—a small trailer—and she and her boyfriend/manager would always eat salads behind the trailer away from everyone else."

"However being the director of photography and having a camera close to her al lot of the time," Wexler continues, "I remember her being always prepared, very focused and when "action" was called, she'd jump into her character and do her thing. She created a persona for that character. I was not intimidated by her, so when "action" was called everyone was into her character and in that respect she was very pleasant to work with." Wexler says that from a camera point of view, Wendy was very interesting to light. "She had angular features and her hair and body; she was never in a bad position photographically and I think she knew that. Her boyfriend was always hovering, saying in her ear, "it's ok, it's ok…""

"There's this famous scene where she's driving the (reform school's) school bus and she bashes the windows out. Then there' s a trucking shot that we filmed in an abandoned airport, where she duplicates climbing out of the window and climbing up to the top of the bus and stands on top of the bus – she did that herself; no stunt woman- and she raises her fist. She had bootstraps that she could secure herself with. We had time for a short rehearsal and she said, "No, I'm fine, I can do this stunt myself" and she created this iconic image of herself standing on top of that bus."

"One of my favorite shots," Wexler says, "is where Wendy's character is dying, lying bloody on the concrete and she says "See you in hell, Edna. [*Edna was the reform school matron in the film, played by Pat Ast*]. That shot was on a cold winter night and I thought we nailed it in terms of the lighting. That shot is sexy, provocative, a little sad. It's always one of my favorite images."

Something curious about *Reform School Girls* is that Wendy was born in 1949, the film was made in 1986 and her character is an inmate at a reform school for teenage girls. When Wendy appears in this film, her real-life age is approximately 37. This works on a level because when the teenage girl inmates act up in the film, Edna always threatens to have their sentences doubled. Perhaps Wendy's character, Charlie Chambliss, was such a troublemaker that her sentence was constantly doubled – so much that she's still an inmate well into her thirties. Or maybe Charlie liked the power she had over the other girls so much that life on the outside wasn't that appealing.

"Hollywood casting has lots of intricacies." says Wexler. "The part was originally written for a male. New Line [*Cinema, Reform School Girls' production company*] probably felt that Wendy had a following and that maybe they could have a built-in-audience."

"We had an awesome First Assistant Director on the set, Kristine Peterson" Wexler says, "and having women behind the scenes gave it a certain vibe. My First Assistant Director was Aggi Lukaszewski who would pull the measuring tape right up to Wendy's nose and Wendy didn't flinch. If a man did that her reaction might have been different."

Wendy's next album, the follow-up to *W.O.W.*, was *Kommander of Kaos*, released by Gigasaurus Records on February 26, 1986. Recorded at the sprawling Broccoli Rabe studios in New Jersey, it was produced by Rod Swenson. "I remember Wendy being very excited about the recording and writing process," says Greg Smith, bassist in *W.O.W.* at the time of *Kommander of Kaos*. "We all were, as it was the first time we got to record in the studio as a band. The writing was done at Wendy and Rod's loft in NYC where we all came together and hashed out ideas and turned them into songs."

The tracks on *Kommander of Kaos*: "Hoy Hey (Live to Rock)" "Goin' Wild," "Party," "Pedal To The Metal," "Ain't None of Your Business, a cover of Motörhead's "Jailbait" "Bad Girl," "Fight for the Right, "and "(Work That Muscle) Fuck That Booty," continue in the pleasure anthem rampage tone that had always been present in Wendy's music and came to full flower in her solo career, e.g. some lyrics of "Goin' Wild" are: "Goin mad/want you so bad/I'm goin'wild."

The cover of *Kommander of Chaos* finds Wendy lying on the hood of a large white car that has just crashed through a wall. This image brings to mind the chrome angel decoration typically found on the front of a Rolls-Royce. But here, Wendy looks more fierce and dangerous than that.

Video of the W.O.W. band playing "Pedal To the Metal" finds Wendy punctuating the lyrics by growling "Wow!" at the song's refrain. By reveling in the exclamatory aspect of her initials this way, Wendy also indulges in a bit of onstage self- promotion (something not exactly forbidden in rock music).

Other footage of Wendy and her band at the time of *Kommander of Kaos* finds Wendy, clad in a black bra, black bikini bottoms and black chaps, doing full backbends while singing, notably during a 1985 performance of the song "Party." Her knees are on the stage and as she bends backward she touches the stage with the top of her head – something only a person in extremely good physical shape could do.

Having a very supportive attitude towards her fans, Wendy exchanged letters with fan Tom Moretti at this time. In one letter to him, she wrote:

10/17/85

Yo Tom,

Just got back from London. One of the gigs we did there was a show called Live From London, beamed throughout Europe, Scandanavia, Japan, Australia. A one-hour concert and we did most the new Kommander of Kaos album.

Lemmy and [Motörhead guitarist] Würzel joined us onstage for "Jailbait!" It was a Killer Show! And the album is the roughest, toughest no bullshit METAL EVER PLAYED! NO FUCKING RADIO SONGS!

January the new album and a video of the London gig will be available in the States! IT WILL KILL YOU!

Fuck n Roll,

XXX

Wendy

P.S. T-Shirts are available through the club, write them

Did you see National Lampoon's Mad as Hell Issue? P. 22

Wendy often wrote Fuck 'n' Roll whenever she signed an autograph.

Footage of Wendy backstage before performing "Going Wild" at a London concert shows her taking a sip from a dainty floral teacup. As she leaves her dressing room and walks to the stage, she beckons the camera towards her and gives it an air kiss.

"I remember playing at CBGB in NYC," Greg Smith says, regarding being in the W.OW. band. "I accidentally slammed myself in the head with my bass and opened it up pretty good. I had a lot of friends at the show and we were going out afterwards. Wendy refused to let me go anywhere till I came back to the loft with her and she cleaned my gashed head with peroxide and put a Band-Aid on it." Ida Langsam also reflects on Wendy's personality: "She didn't gossip about people. She was friends with all the musicians that worked with her. I think she was very kind to them."

(After leaving *W.O.W.*, Greg Smith has played with bands such as Rainbow, Blue Öyster Cult, Alan Parsons, Alice Cooper and Billy Joel. He has been playing bass with Ted Nugent since 2006.)

In *W.O.W.* Wendy had left behind her shaving cream, electrical tape and Mohawk in terms of her performance comportment. Fronting the band named for her initials, she was often clad in a black bra and bikini bottoms, sweat glazing her extremely fit and toned body.

Wendy sometimes sat her guitarist or bassist on her shoulders, demonstrating how fit and strong she was. In *W.O.W.* her presence was very physical, sexual and fierce, as if she was turning her onstage focus inward, expressing herself *through* herself and not through objects as she did before. Although in *W.O.W.* she would sometimes chainsaw a guitar or something a bit more unusual, as sound engineer Lance C. Phillips recalls: "The *W.O.W.* album tour happened at the height of the Boy George sensation, so we had a faux Boy George doll that Wendy would chainsaw in half. That was the only theatrical aspect of the *W.O.W.* tour. I think there was some chainsawing of guitars and whatnot. It was almost anticlimactic really, it was like 'they expect to see something get destroyed so let's at least give them this.' But it was much more straightforward music oriented."

Wendy filmed a public service announcement about safe sex in 1985 for U68, the UHF music video channel broadcasting in the New York City area. Clad in a black leather motorcycle jacket and black bra, her blonde hair framing her face, Wendy looks at the camera and emphatically says: "Sex is one of the best things we've got going, but venereal disease can kill ya. So remember; if it's not clean enough to put it in your mouth, don't take it home and sleep with it."

"I did sound for Wendy O. at a Rock Hotel show at Irving Plaza in the mid-eighties, 1985 or so" says Mick Oakleaf, New York based musician and audio technician. "Chris Williamson was the promoter and man in charge of Rock Hotel. He had a record label too. I was the stage monitor mixer for her show. She sawed a TV propped on a bar stool to bits with a freaking gas-powered chainsaw. I knew she was going to do it but it was a lot more destructive than I thought it would be. The bits flew everywhere and I ducked under the monitor console to avoid the flying glass. The console got a careful vacuuming the next day!

"I hung out with her a bit before the show," Oakleaf recalls, "and she seemed totally opposite to the way she was onstage – very reserved an mild mannered. She seemed very intelligent and nice."

"Wendy was a truly nice, caring person," says Pete Capadoccia, "Very funny to be around. She took her role as a singer and as a spokesperson for her war on conformity very seriously. She wanted to empower women. She honestly wanted the world to be a better place. She liked to make people question the norm. She loved it when people would be all freaked out about her look and her wild woman image. Then she would talk to them and they would be dumb founded that she was a very smart and articulate woman that was truly passionate about what she was doing. She loved it when people would realize that she was a real person and got past the hype that surrounded her. Everything she did was in an effort to make others open their minds and think."

Wendy posed for a *Playboy* pictorial for the men's magazine's October 1986 issue. When contacted by Jeff Cohen, *Playboy*'s managing photo editor at that time, about being photographed for *Playboy*, Wendy turned the offer down a few times. Then, when

Cohen said "We'll do something really outrageous," Wendy was more enthusiastic about the proposition. "I'd love to do a pictorial," she said. "I have lists of things I always wanted to do, so I'll give you number one: I'm gonna walk on the wing of a plane. At 400 feet. Naked." *Playboy* gave Wendy's concept the go-ahead, with Rod Swenson as producer of the shoot. But as Cohen remembers "Unfortunately the photographers Rod hired had technical difficulties which resulted in very little useable film. I remember being totally bummed but obviously there would be no reshoots on an assignment of this scale."

Although Wendy did walk on the wing of an antique plane flying over Mexico, and parachute off the plane's wing, the photographs of her performing this stunt aren't the focus of the pictorial – there's only two small pictures of Wendy on the wing of the plane and jumping. Instead, the larger full-page pictorial photographs show her fairly nude with her bikini area waxed, clad in just a harness or chaps, straddling a propeller or lying on a parachute. As Arny Freytag, who photographed the pictorial explains: "It would be very difficult to photograph her nude while wing walking so we decided to design the shoot as if she had parachuted from the airplane. This allowed us to have a background that tied in the wing walk idea with a sexy environment."

In Wendy's pictorial she doesn't look exceptionally different from how she looks when performing circa 1986, except for the full frontal nudity (her black electrical tape is clearly a thing of the past). The photographs, by Freytag, don't show Wendy with a faux ecstatic expression on her face like typical women in *Playboy* layouts. In quite a few of the photos, Wendy is turned away from the camera – a regard that could possibly be interpreted as challenging the male gaze. "When we did celebrity pictorials we were not trying to copy our Playmate feature look," says Freytag. "When we photographed Playmates there was a certain look we wanted to project. However when we shot other features for the magazine we were not restricted to the "Playmate" look or style of photography. Plus I think it fitted with her personality."

In the photos Wendy has a certain relaxed seriousness to her. In one photograph, her back is to the camera and she's pulling at what looks like either spider or cobwebs (perhaps because it's *Playboy*'s October issue, nodding to Halloween). According to a 2016 report in *The Irish Times*, Tadgh O'Cuinn, a great Gaelic physician of the middle ages, once wrote that "the spider's web, cold and dry, it has the retentive virtue. It stops the bleeding of wounds and it heals."

"Wendy was a lot of fun to work with," says Freytag, "and being a performer she was professional and loved the camera. I always thought photographing performers was much easier than models or amateur models like Playmates. They "perform" for the camera."

The idea of Wendy posing nude for *Playboy* toes the line between unexpected and expected. On one hand she built a career while performing quasi topless and being unabashedly sexual onstage in an iconoclastic manner, so the idea of her posing nude would seem to suit her image. On the other, a woman celebrity posing nude for Playboy is somewhere between selling out and cashing in on her sexuality—there's something very typical and mainstream about doing such a thing. Yet Wendy had never been a "snob" regarding the media – the Plasmatics appeared on network television shows gladly, for instance.

Peppering the un-bylined article accompanying the pictorial in *Playboy* are candid quotes from Wendy, reflecting on what it means to be her:

"I'm an urban guerilla who loves roarin', wailin', and rattlin' my insides, but when it comes to my band, I'm a dictator – a real ball buster. So I hire only people who put their music before everything else."

"I go through musicians like I go through cars."

"I'm an adrenaline freak. But before I perform a stunt I can't talk, I can't eat. I can't do anything. I'm nuts – I'm outta my mind."

"I don't hesitate. Before a concert, I'll appear calm and quiet, and then suddenly, I'll explode."

"The only thing that pulled me across that wing was fucking desire. I was an animal working on instinct. My mind was out the window."

"Being dragged around with the wind beating on me was one of the most sensuous feelings in the world – a real rush. See, I've got a real tight body, so the wind wasn't painful. In fact it was a real turn-on. It's sort of like fucking: You can tell people about fucking but they won't understand till they actually do it…"

The writer asks her "How turned on were you Wendy? Did you want to jump your boyfriend the minute you touched down – from a 1200 foot free fall."

"You mean, did it make me horny? I'm *always* horny," she replies.

"It was gorgeous up there," she said. "The photographers were sweatin' and I was grooving."

"I have dreams at night that I'm flying – that I step off a building or something and I actually fly. So I wake up with this feeling that stays with me all day. I want everybody to get off on the pictures as much as I got off doing the stunt."

The writer then concludes "And then with a shrug, she added 'It's great to get off.'"

In the 1980s, Wendy appeared several times on *Night Flight*, the USA Network music show, both on the *Night Flight* and *Radio 1990* programs. Wendy interviewed Motley Crüe members Vince Neil and Tommy Lee on Night Flight's *Radio 1990* program in 1985. Wendy announces that it's "heavy metal Wednesday" and introduces Neil and Lee the as the "bad boys of rock 'n' roll – or should I say the two *darlings* of rock 'n' roll." Clad in her trademark black leather bra and a pair of faded jeans, Wendy is smiling and comfortable during the interview, which begins with the Crüe members introducing their "first-ever video" for their song "Live Wire," and Wendy complimenting Lee on a new tattoo.

Around this time, Neil had been arrested in a drunk driving accident where Razzle (nee Charles Dingley) the drummer from glam metal band Hanoi Rocks had been killed and two others had been permanently injured. Wendy brings up this subject in a very tactful manner, telling Neil that she knows he can't discuss the circumstances but asks him to talk about his true feelings and also about their new album, *Theatre of Pain*.

Neil then talks about wanting to inform their fans about the dangers of drunk driving and how "even though we're the bad boys of rock, it doesn't mean that we don't care about people." In June of 1986, Neil would serve a jail sentence for the drunk driving charge that he would later remark was "too short."

Certain Internet sources claim that during Motley Crüe's 1982 New Year's Eve concert at the Santa Monica Civic Center, the band brought a mannequin onstage that was made to look like Wendy and beheaded it. Wendy doesn't mention this to Neil and Lee during the *Radio 1990* interview. Instead she is friendly to them during the conversation where Neil talks about using pentagrams to enhance the Motley Crüe brand, the band's upcoming tour plans and then he and Lee discuss how beautiful they think Swedish girls are.

On the *Joan Rivers Show* in 1986, Wendy and Joan are enthusiastically chit-chatting like old girlfriends. Wendy is clad in a black leather bra and skintight black pants. Rivers asks Wendy where she gets her clothes and Wendy breezily replies, "I just wear what's comfortable." She suggests to Rivers that they get tattoos together and Rivers tells Wendy that's a great idea. When Wendy performs "Goin' Wild" on the show with her band she seems far removed from her TV-destroying Mohawk and black electrical tape days. In performances of her solo era, Wendy comes across as more of a metallic hard rocker, blissfully banging her head in a black bikini. In certain W.O.W. performances, Wendy would at times carry a band member on her shoulders while he played guitar, proving how strong her body was.

Wendy had acquired a number of tattoos circa this time: a rose on one arm with the words "I Love Sex and Rock 'n' Roll" – the title of one of the songs on *W.O.W* – and later, the mythological South American winged serpent Quetzocoatl wrapping around her forearm under the logo for *W.O.W.* near her shoulder. On her back, was etched a large winged creature with a snake in its mouth stepping on what looks like cactus framed by the words United Federation of the Universe.

"I didn't want to leave anyone out," Wendy remarked to Joan Rivers during an appearance on the comedienne's Fox network talk show, when she discussed this back tattoo during her interview segment.

In videos of certain *W.O.W.* performances, audience members jump on stage, something that didn't typically happen when the Plasmatics played. Perhaps this was because the *W.O.W.* band was performing rock music that wasn't quite as confrontationally alien as the Plasmatics'. Maybe the –typically male—audience members at *W.O.W.* concerts saw Wendy and her accompanying musicians as fitting more within the frame of metal, where stage diving was expected behavior.

1987 saw the Plasmatics reforming to an extent on *Maggots: The Album*. The band on the *Maggots* album consisted of three members of the Plasmatics: Wendy on vocals, Wes Beech on lead guitar, rhythm guitar and backing vocals, who had been a Plasmatic since the time right before *New Hope For The Wretched*, Chris Romanelli on bass and backing vocals who joined the Plasmatics at the time of the *Metal Priestess* EP, and Michael Ray, from Wendy's solo band on rhythm guitar, lead guitar and backing vocals and drummer Ray Callahan, a recent addition to this lineup. *Maggots* marks the final recorded appearance of a form of the Plasmatics on an album with Wendy. On the cover, Wendy's name appears above a Plasmatics logo.

Maggots: The Album released in 1987 by Profile Records in the U.S. and the GWR label in other countries, is a concept album – nee a "thrash opera," about global warming recorded many years before the melting of polar ice caps and other types of environmental peril seeped into everyday consciousness. *Maggots* consists of heavy, metallic songs sung by Wendy, interspersed with actors speaking dialogue telling of the disintegration of both the fictional and dysfunctional White family and the Earth. On the *Maggots* album, scientists intending to solve the problem of pollution create a retrovirus intended to consume ocean and river trash, but flooding that comes about because of global warming puts the virus in contact with common maggots. These maggots then double in size. They constantly look for things to consume, laying waste to cities and

eating people. There is no turning back as "civilization" is destroyed
– brought about by its own over consumption and disregard for the
environment. This story, portrayed by voice actors, is played out
through the falling apart White family who get devoured by giant
maggots while watching a TV game show. As critic Craig Curtice
wrote in an AllMusic.com review: "More of an audio play than a
music album, a Rod Serling-like narrator takes listeners through a
disturbingly graphic story depicting genetically mutated maggots
breeding exponentially until mankind is exterminated."

In the artwork for the album there's a photo of Wendy holding a
mock newspaper bearing the headline: "THOSE WHO ARE
EATING WILL SOON BE EATEN." Another slogan used at this
time is "The Day of the Humans is Gone." This is a prescient
statement about the connection between meat consumption and
global warming. In 2019, when Greta Thunberg angrily railed and
wept in front of the UN General Assembly about being robbed of her
future because of their inaction regarding climate change, a large
section of the Amazon rainforest was set on fire to create cattle
grazing land. Animal flatulence has been linked to the depletion of
the ozone layer as well. As Craig Curtice goes on to say in his
AllMusic review: "Once tossed off as gory camp, realized
environmental changes and threats of biological terrorism made this
prophetic release particularly unnerving."

Kerrang! gave *Maggots* a rave review – lauding it with five Ks;
the hard rock/heavy metal magazine's highest praise. Calling it "quite
simply a work of genius."

Mike Schnapp, the Plasmatics fan who was in the audience of the
Tomorrow show appearance by the band was working in the music
industry at this time and seized an opportunity to work for the
Plasmatics by promoting *Maggots* in 1987. "I worked as a promotion
person directly for Rod Swenson," Schnapp said in a 2020 interview.
"He had heard of me and called me directly. I didn't know who he
was. He called up and said, 'Hey I'm Rod Swenson—Plasmatics. We
have this record called *Maggots* and we want to hire you to do radio
promotion for the band and for the record. I said, "Cool, ok." So I
worked out of the Second Vision offices which was downtown on

Crosby and Howard Streets *[in NYC]*. That became Caroline Records headquarters.

"I was there for two months and I would call all these radio stations and we mailed out the record. I'd call and say, "Did you get the record? Did you listen to it? Could you play it? Could you do an interview or a contest?" That's what you do as a promotion person.

"At that point I was doing hard rock, heavy metal radio – it wasn't like I was reaching out to WKTU, the disco station, I wasn't calling WPLJ, the regular rock 'n' roll station. I was calling these extreme radio stations and a lot of them just had shows and you'd have like an hour, whether it was college radio or it was Fingers at WBAB or Cheryl and Eddie at WDHA where it was a commercial hard rock radio station and on Saturday night at midnight they have their metal show where they play all the crazy shit. *Maggots* was definitely lumped into the crazy shit. A), it's the Plasmatics and B), this Plasmatics record was innovative because on each side they had three or four songs and in between the songs they had a dialogue and it was like a horror film. It was a combination horror film and horror film soundtrack."

There was a record release party for *Maggots: The Album* at The Palladium in New York City. By 1987, The Palladium had been converted from the cavernous venue where the Plasmatics first blew up a car in 1979 and a slew of rock bands had since performed, to an arty hotspot transformed by Steve Rubell and Ian Schrager, who created Studio 54. During this record release party, Wendy tore apart a typical American living room with a chainsaw and a sledgehammer, echoing previous statements she made about refusing to be middle class.

One might wonder as to what sort of reception a concept record like *Maggots* would get at radio, but according to Schnapp, promoting it via niche heavy metal programs was the right move.

"I don't know how it charted I don't remember any facts or figures but the stations definitely played the record. I brought Wendy and Rod out to some stations to do live interviews. I remember driving out to Dover, New Jersey late at night to WDHA because they had a late night radio show on Saturday nights, bringing them out to go live on the air to play some of the music and for Wendy to do an interview live on the air.

As Schnapp remembers, "I vividly remember that they would do a giveaway where they would bring a piece of a guitar that Wendy had chainsawed on stage while it was plugged in. Obviously Rod kept pieces of these guitars and he was smart…Rod's a very smart man, pleasant, rock 'n' roll – what a guy, really a wonderful individual, and he was smart enough to bring those. These radio stations do giveaways but who's giving away a piece of a guitar? You give away an album but also you give away a piece of a guitar, it's a one-of-a-kind collector's item."

Schnapp also recalls Wendy doing something at these radio appearances that she had done onstage with W.O.W. "Wendy would give the DJ a shoulder ride," Schnapp recalls. "Cheryl at WDHA didn't want one but one of the guys, I forget who, they ended up on Wendy's shoulders -- not on her back like a chicken fight, but sitting, like ass on her shoulders and Wendy would stand up…and Wendy wasn't 6'4" she wasn't that tall. So this lady who wasn't very tall, picking a guy up and walking around the radio station with a guy on her shoulders. Quite the feat of strength!"

Bill Lindsey, lead singer of Minneapolis-St. Paul-based shock rock band Impaler, was a big fan of Wendy and the Plasmatics at this time. "When we got signed to Combat Records, Mick Schnapp was the PR guy there and he really helped us. He was one of our best friends in the business because he did a lot for us—got us in different magazines and helped set up shows in other states we hadn't been to before.

"After Schnapp left Combat, he started working for Profile and knew how much I loved the Plasmatics. He was working with Wendy O. and the Plasmatics when they did the *Maggots* album," Lindsey says.

"The first Impaler album was called *Rise Of The Mutants*," Lindsay continues, "and it had kind of a zombie vibe for the cover art, where I'm hunkered over a casket and I have beef liver hanging out of my mouth and stage blood like I'm disemboweling a corpse.

"One day I was in my apartment in West St. Paul and the phone rings. I pick it up and I hear "Heeeeyy! Liver breath Bill!!! This is

Wendy O. Williams from Plasmatics!" Lindsey was delighted to get this call from Wendy.

"It was me talking a lot and her saying "thank you" a lot. I told her how much the Plasmatics meant to us and how I'd seen them at Duffy's – a small club in Minneapolis and that I'd seen them with KISS. I just told her how great they were. So she called me liver breath bill," he says with a little laugh.

On the tour for the *Maggots* album, Wendy and the Plasmatics were scheduled to play Minneapolis at the First Avenue club – a venue that became famous worldwide when it was featured in the Prince film *Purple Rain*. "The First Avenue club got in touch with me and asked me if Impaler wanted to open for Plasmatics there. Of course we did!" Recalls Lindsey. " I was a tad bit disappointed that Richie Stotts, who I loved a lot, wasn't involved with that tour and it was kind of her solo band. But the thing that was really cool was that Wes Beech was involved in that tour. He was at sound check and we talked to him for 45 minutes and that was so great to meet and talk to him."

As Lindsey remembers, Wendy did not come to sound check for the First Avenue show. As he explains: "The thing that really stuck out in my mind was that a roadie did the sound check and the vocals but he sounded *exactly* like her! He did a good imitation of her and they put some effects on the voice but it sounded like she was doing that sound check. So that was really crazy. She didn't come to the club till after we were onstage, so I didn't really get to talk to her at the show but I got to talk to Wes and see Plasmatics again. That was probably the third or fourth time I got to see them."

The *Maggots* album being very high concept and a compelling blend of aural and visual, Lindsey was asked what the Plasmatics show was like that night. "Wendy's always visual but it wasn't to the extent that of the early Plasmatics. It was more straightforward like her solo show had been where she just came out and performed and was high energy. First Avenue has screens and I remember some stock footage of maggots squirming around. They had a big backdrop of the *Maggots* album cover, that's how that was represented."

Bill Batson was a sound engineer for Wendy and the Plasmatics that night. "I did stage monitors at the First Avenue club when the

Plasmatics played there on the Maggots tour, 1987 thereabouts," he says.

"I was told by the band and the road manager not to worry about the band to just to follow Wendy. I had ten monitor mixes across the front of the stage and I would just feed her voice as she ran across the stage into each monitor mix as she goes and turning it down as she left. I spent an hour to 45 minutes doing that. She went back and forth the like an aerobics teacher on a pogo stick.

"It was a great performance," Batson recalls "after she goes offstage, the tour manager says to me 'Wendy wants to see you right now!' and I think, 'Oh, fuck! What the hell?' So I go backstage and she says to me 'These are the best fuckin' monitors I've had for the whole tour!" And she pulls off her tee shirt and throws it at my face and then puts shaving creem or Reddi-Whip on her tits and goes back out and does a 15 minute encore."

"It was a very rowdy crowd that night and they really loved her," Batson says.

"I thought Wendy was a great show-person and a big influence. I thought it was so cool that she was an animal rights activist and a vegetarian, and she was just such a gentle person," Lindsey recalls. "I really admired that about her--of course all the music and everything they created with the Plasmatics. It's funny because in my career I'm the singer in a shock rock band but I work in a hospital and a lot of people are shocked that this guy with liver hanging out of his mouth actually takes care of people. I feel a kind of kinship with her in that sense. I'm a vegetarian too. I loved that about her and she was a very intelligent person, so well spoken."

"I was really crushed the day she died. It was sad to lose a hero," says Lindsey.

Around the time of *Maggots*' release, Wendy hosted the second episode of *Headbanger's Ball* – MTV's heavy metal show. Mike Schapp gives some background to the genesis of the show and Wendy's appearance on it "In 1985 MTV had a once a month show called *Metal Mania* hosted by Dee Snider. I became friendly with Dee Snider through that – great guy, really into promoting the scene he was in. He's really visual and he's got the passion for it. So I got

Megadeth's first mention on MTV when they didn't have a video. Right before their first record came out I just gave them their logo and tour dates. So Dee talked about their tour dates and put their logo up-that was the first mention of Megadeth on MTV. Cut to 1987 I'm working Wendy O. and MTV has this new show called *Headbanger's Ball*. Motörhead may have just been the first band that was booked. I had just worked Motörhead so I knew that. Then Wendy got booked for the second episode."

Schnapp explains how Wendy's appearance on *Headbangers' Ball* to promote *Maggots* was rather unique: "They did a green screen where she stands in front of footage of maggots – I don't know how Rod Swenson got this, god bless him -the whole background. Real maggots are really disgusting – this is no rock 'n' roll trick this is no pyrotechnics. This is real science footage of real maggots crawling around; the whole background."

"Rod Swenson is one of the greatest geniuses I've ever met," says Schnapp. "He knew what rock 'n' roll was, what was artistic and what was shocking. He was really great to work with. He was soft-spoken, he didn't yell and scream. He was intelligent, succinct and to the point."

As Wendy announces metal music videos behind a desk, she alternately displays a white electric guitar that's a contest prize, talks about another contest were the winner gets to appear in a video for the band Keel, and folds her arms and collapses with her head on the desk.

(Since his days working for Rod and Wendy, Schnapp went on to act in several films, be resident DJ at New York nightclub Bungalow 8 and be an Associate Producer for the documentary *Rolling Stone: The Life and Death of Brian Jones)*

Also in 1987, Wendy had a role on *The New Adventures of Beans Baxter*. A show on the Fox network about a teenage boy, played by Jonathan Ward, who's a spy as an "after school job."

In 1988, Wendy released her last album– a fusion of rock and hip-hop titled *Deffest! and Baddest!* Initially under the name Utrafly and the Hometown Girls. Still under contract to Profile Records (who released *Maggots*) Profile was known as a hip-hop label as they released the groundbreaking album *Raising Hell* by Run-DMC. The Hometown Girls were Katrina Astrin, a guitarist for the Wisconsin-based all-girl band The Hunted, who had been the opening act for some Plasmatics shows in the Midwest, and LaDonna Sullivan who had travelled with the band and sold t-shirts. According to the official Plasmatics website, Wendy and Rod intended Ultrafly and The Hometown girls to be a fresh concept, bringing additional vocals (by Katrina and LaDonna) and guitar playing by women (by Katrina).Wendy's name was not going to be associated with *Deffest! And Baddest!* but Profile balked at this idea and Wendy's name was placed on the cover art.

The main image of the cover is a peeled banana with a bite taken out of it covered in opaque, beige-ish white liquid – Bechamel sauce? Melted vanilla ice cream? Semen? It's hard to say. Perhaps the cover image is a tweak of the iconic Andy Warhol –designed cover art for The Velvet Underground and Nico album featuring just an image of a banana.

With songs written by Rod Swenson and Wes Beech and the recording produced by Rod, *Deffest! and Baddest!* has an imaginitave playfulness lyrically as well as in its musical blend of rock guitar riffs and turntable scrathing. This album has been referred to as "thrash rap," which seems like a fitting description. It opens with "Rulers of Rock," where Wendy and the Hometown Girls engage in the kind of bragging hip-hop had come to be known for. They boast of having "no sprayed hair/no Spandex." Given that this was recorded during the height of the hair metal era – a genre rife with sexism--a declarative statement like this, coming from women, is boldly assertive.

Wendy raps with a commanding, seductive yet strong flow on "10,000,000 Winner" where she spins the tale of Suzanne, a young virgin whose multimillionaire boyfriend takes her to Paris and buys her *beacoup* amounts of plastic surgery with strange results. Wendy, Katrina and LaDonna berate a macho meathead on "Super Jock Guy." "Early Days" finds Wendy's characteristic rasp returning as she raps about her travels. "On the IRT " describes a New York City subway train transforming into a fantasyland and rhymes "giddy" with "G.Gordon Liddy." "La La Land" chronicles the goings-on at a wild Beverly Hills party where Shirley MacLaine, "dressed as a man" greets Wendy by saying "om shanti." Also present at this Hollywood fete are headline makers of the day such as Jerry Falwell, Jessica Hahn and Gary Hart. On "Lies" Wendy's gritty vocals mesh very well with Katrina and LaDonna's as they decry falsehoods stemming from corporations, the media, cosmetics companies and other sources of society's ills."The Humpty Song," finds Wendy putting a spin on a nursery rhyme as Astrin and Sullivan chant "When you're up you're up/and when you're down you're down," fates that happen to everyday people, not just giant eggs.

Kerrang! (who always seemed to be in Wendy's corner, critically) praised *Deffest! and Baddest!,* calling the album: "Screaming Bleeding Grinding Klassic Lyrics For Klassic Times. Get it!" This praise appeared on the album's cover, diagonally across from its parental advisory sticker.

There was a tour for *Deffest! and Baddest!* in 1988. It would be Wendy's last.

In a video interview from 1988, Wendy is lounging back on a sofa clad in leather pants that zip up the side, a black bra and a leather harness across her chest. In contrast to her tough-chick attire, she has an aura of polite sweetness as she agreeably answers the interviewer's questions with a warm, constant smile. At one point during the interview, a member of the crew asks Wendy to refrain from repeatedly lightly slapping her left leather-clad knee because it's creating noise and she affably complies.

The interviewer asks Wendy's opinion of "women rockers" and she talks about Bessie Smith with a tone of reverence. He then asks her what she thinks of The Supremes, "with their opera gloves and evening gowns…" as he puts it.

"Oh, I think they're great," Wendy responds glowingly.

In 1989, Wendy had a rather scene-stealing role in *Pucker Up And Bark Like a Dog*, an independent film directed by Paul S. Parco. It's a romantic comedy with an emphasis on comedy, set in contemporary Los Angeles. The film stars actors Jon Gries (who was also in

Napoleon Dynamite and *Men in Black*) and Lisa Zane as Max and Taylor, two twentysomethings having no luck getting their careers nor their relationship off the ground. Max is a shy artist who can't get any gallery owners interested in his paintings and Taylor is an actress having a difficult time getting cast in any role. Even though they're attracted to each other all sorts of circumstances thwart them from being happy together.(Other notable actors appearing in the film are Phyllis Diller, Paul Bartel, Isabel Sanford and Robert Culp.)

One night, Max is so despondent that he lies in the street after having too much to drink, bemoaning his loser status. Along comes Wendy on a motorcycle, playing a biker chick character named Butch. (According to a crew member of *Pucker Up..* Wendy did not know how to ride a motorcycle and had to be pushed into the frame of this scene.) After taking a swig from Max's fifth of liquor (a true bit of acting for Wendy because she never drank alcohol) and throwing the bottle, which breaks, Max says to Butch "Women suck…art sucks…my life sucks." Butch rolls her eyes and says "Men suck *worse*."

Despite this, she takes a shine to Max. Butch takes him for a ride on her bike as the Plasmatics' "Doom Song" plays over zooming shots of the L.A. roadways. Then Butch and Max are seen at a a burger joint where Wendy is truly acting again--eating what at least seems to be a hamburger. (Wendy didn't eat meat.)

Over burgers, Butch declares to Max that, because he's "the only guy to ride with me over 160 and not vomit and you haven't been a pain in the ass," she's going to fuck him. Max is rather flummoxed by this. They go to Max's very industrial looking one-story apartment building. Butch can't wait to get inside as she demands that Max undress. ("Shouldn't we maybe have a drink first?" Max suggests weakly). In the vestibule of Max's apartment building, Butch – lashing at the walls around him with a leather whip—continues to demand that Max take his clothes off. He does doff his shirt. "Are you man enough to act like a dog?" Butch says tormentingly to Max.

Taylor arrives at the glass door of the vestibule at this very inopportune time. Seeing Wendy – wearing just a black bra and tight pants – brandishing her whip around a bare-chested Max, Taylor flees. Max rushes out after her but she's gone. Consoling Max, Butch gives the keys for her bike to him so he can go after Taylor, warning him that if he damages "her machine" she'll take off all his skin with a safety razor. She asks Max for the keys to his apartment so she can "catch some zzzs." He obliges and gives Butch a kiss on the cheek as he hurries out of the building.

Wendy appeared on an episode of *MacGyver* that aired on November 5, 1990 as the demanding accomplice of an inept bikeresque robber. He quite literally jumps the gun in his attempt to rob McGyver (played by original series star Richard Dean Anderson), co-star Abe Vigoda and a two nuns—he forgot to bring his gun. Instead he's pointing his index fingers and telling them to give him an expensive piece of jewelry. Wendy comes through the doorway, pointing a gun at MacGyver and company. Wearing jeans and a black leather halter, Wendy's hair hangs down her back in a braid with her blonde bangs hanging near her eyes. She exhales heavily, wisping her bangs out of her eyes. "Can't you wait!!" She admonishes the goofy biker guy, as she brandishes the gun, "All right! Hand it over," she commands, "Nowww!" in a growl very similar to her onstage vocal style.

In a later scene taking place at an ice rink, Wendy's character holds a nun at gunpoint as she and her inept biker boyfriend demand "the real thing this time," as their fence said the jewels they got from the previous scene were fake.

"Play it straight! Or say goodbye to the penguin!" Wendy snarls at MacGyver as she points her gun at the nun. MacGyver says "ok" but proceeds to whack the jewels towards Wendy across the ice with a hockey stick. Wendy doesn't catch them. What ensues is a melee on the ice where Wendy tussles with said nun and bangs her head against the rink's wall.

The acting roles Wendy got in film and TV seem to be in line with her onstage persona during the W.O.W. era. Usually playing tough women and clad in attire similar to what she wore when singing with her band, it could be said that she was typecast as herself. Although it would have been highly unlikely to see Wendy on an episode of *Full House*, actors who can play a range of roles tend to get more acting work.

Walking Away

In 1991, Wendy and Rod moved to Storrs, Connecticut, where, at The University of Connecticut, Rod took a lecturer's position and became a fellow at the Center for Ecological Study of Perception and Action. He went on to be published in several scientific journals for his research on the laws of evolution, thermodynamics, and entropy. Rod built a geodesic home for them in the woods near Storrs.

Wendy stopped performing altogether at this point. If she was looking to completely distance herself from the persona she had created as frontwoman for the Plasmatics, living in Storrs was as far as she could get – perhaps to her detriment. As Ida Langsam states, "It would seem to me that she was fed up with the industry. They didn't treat her very well. I was shocked when she killed herself. Maybe Connecticut was too quiet for her. Maybe she wanted to get away and it was just too far away."

In the 1990s, Storrs was a very rural and picturesque town in Northeastern Connecticut, not very densely populated outside of the UCONN campus. It had an overall sleepy, isolated and peaceful atmosphere. There's no train station connecting Storrs to any other big East Coast city -- just a bus.

Marisha Chinsky, a New York City-based public relations professional, grew up in Storrs in the 1990s. As she describes the town: "Storrs was inhabited by a lot of farmers, nature lovers, university faculty and their families, and largely progressive liberal hippie-types. Some people owned horses and built lakes on their properties. (Trick or treating was a fruitless effort since a child might make it to 5 houses in a few hours but you'd get $1 from each house. Christmas caroling in town was a bit more productive!). The nearest city was Hartford, which is not - and never has been- the most lively or exciting or full of culture. Hartford is mostly a financial center full of insurance company office buildings. Therefore, people in Storrs clung to their quiet, natural way of life and might travel to Providence, Rhode Island or Boston for the nearest city culture. Going north to Northampton or Amherst, Massachusetts was another nearby getaway for a more vibrant college town (the East Village of New England, I called it which is a very 90s statement given how bland the EV is today). There is one college radio station in Storrs, WHUS. The local health food store is the Willimantic Food Co-op, which is the next town over from Storrs and Mansfield. I never went there but it is very popular and well-loved by students especially. I think it functions like a traditional co-op with volunteer shifts for members."

Helen Scanlon, Women's Affairs Director at local college radio station WHUS, Remembers Wendy as blonde, dressed simply in leggings and a shirt. "She was a tiny wisp of a person, with a sweet voice and always with a smile. She rode her bike all over town," Scanlon says.

Kevin White was Wendy and Rod's insurance representative in Storrs. According to him, Rod and Wendy lived in a house they built on a quiet street. "My first contact with Rod was when he needed a bond to build his driveway." White says Rod and Wendy's home "wasn't extravagant" and had a modern design and a modest size. He talked with Wendy the day before her suicide. "She seemed normal," he says, adding that she called to make some routine inquiries about her auto policy. "But nothing that would have indicated she was 'tidying' up loose ends," he says. White thought just the opposite, as Wendy talked about the impact of the changes she was making on future payments.

"I don't know if local folks knew about Wendy's days in the Plasmatics," White continues, "Certainly her off stage demeanor wouldn't have lent any indication. I knew, because I was in the music biz myself after college, and my roommate was Brian Battles, of WCCC, who introduced Wendy and the Plasmatics at Stage West and other local larger event venues that were around back then. My interactions with her found her relatively soft spoken, and kind of along the lines of a nature loving – call it "Crunchy Granola" down to earth type."

"I remember her," says Meg Heffley-Brauch, a horse trainer in Storrs. "She used to come in to *(Danbury, Connecticut pet store)* Puppy Love all the time. She was quiet and did a lot of rehabilitation with squirrels. I worked there from 1995-1997. She came in a lot to buy supplies for the animals and I remember we had her business card behind the counter. She worked at the Willimantic Food Co-op back in the 1990s. I remember her riding her bike up and down."

Wendy volunteered at the Willimantic Food Co-op in exchange for a store discount. Co-op general manager Alice Rubin recalls Wendy riding an old fashioned bicycle to the co-op and often wearing a flannel shirt and leggings with her hair in braids or pigtails. Rubin recalls Wendy making kanten pudding (kanten is the Japanese word for agar-agar, a very low calorie gelatinous substance derived from algae) that Wendy handed out samples and recipes for. "She might have done other things as well," Rubin says, "but that was what I remember her for." With regards to Wendy's past as a famous rock star, Rubin reflects: "I don't think that many people really knew who she was, or if they did, they didn't make a big deal about it."

Wendy also worked at the Parkade Health Shoppe, between Storrs and Hartford. All the employees there were required to wear white lab coats. Like the other workers at Parkade, Wendy was helpful and smiling. She knew a lot about vitamins.

But there was something troubling Wendy and she was often late for work at Parkade. Eventually she was fired. Parkade tried to deny her unemployment benefits and she was upset about that.

She volunteered at the Quiet Corner Wildlife Center where injured and abandoned animals were eased back into the wild. As Joy Williams wrote in SPIN Magazine: "You didn't look into the animals' eyes, you didn't make pets of them." Wendy didn't believe in pets; she thought they were prisoners.

At one point Wendy distanced herself from Swenson and became romantically involved with Steve Gabriel, a tattoo artist in East Hartford. She moved in with him in September of 1997. He was working on redoing her tattoos into an intricate fire-and-water rendering he came up with. According to Roger Catlin in *The*

Hartford Courant, Wendy was hoping this new tattoo would help her get cast in a Fox production but that didn't happen.

At this time, Wendy tried to get some publicity for Gabriel by using her celebrity status to bring attention to his tattooing. She was interviewed by Jayne Keedle, reporter for the *Hartford Advocate* but Wendy asked Keedle to hold the story as her relationship with Gabriel started to unravel.

She reportedly wanted to move back in with Rod Swenson and repeatedly called him. She was unhappy about the tattoos. She had wanted leopard spots but Gabriel couldn't do them.

"I have this one memory that really stands out," says Helen Scanlon, "I was working at the Willimantic Food Co-op, I'd say 1995. I had seen Wendy riding her bike around town and shopping at the Co-op and I was always fascinated by her--I mean, she was Wendy O. Williams--but I had never formally met her. Then, one day, she came into the Co-op, and she had something in her shirt pocket. I had approached her and asked what she had--and she very gently opened her shirt pocket, leaned in so I could see better, and there was a tiny baby squirrel curled up taking a nap. I said, "Thank you Wendy for caring for this little guy. He looks very happy and healthy." She offered me a big smile. We then continued marveling at the squirrel baby in her pocket as other Co-op staff gathered around to get a glimpse of the little creature. She was like a proud mother, happy to share the squirrel baby with those who wanted a peek. If I remember correctly, she had brought some formula and an eye dropper to make sure her charge was properly nourished as she went about her day. She was a gentle, caring soul--long blonde hair tied back, dressed simply in leggings and sneakers. Her voice was sweet and quiet, and to us--she was simply "Wendy." When she was at the Co-op, it was "hi Wendy" from the staff, and she always smiled in return. She liked being there, and we always enjoyed seeing her. I remember her smile most of all."

But the peace and quiet of Storrs didn't quell Wendy's troubles during the `90s, a decade where she felt out of place in the pop culture sphere.

In 1992, Sinead O'Connor tore up a photo of Pope John Paul II on Saturday Night Live and it resulted in a huge headline-grabbing scandal that deflated the Irish singer's career in the U.S. This incident, plus the slavishly uncritical yellow-ribbons-everywhere attitude mainstream America had towards the Persian Gulf War and the controversy over explicit content in music resulted in a cultural climate unwelcoming for iconoclasts at that time. Appearing on the TV talk show *Donahue* in 1990, as part of a program discussing music censorship (alongside outspoken punk activist Jello Biafra and Luther Campbell from the extremely explicit rap group 2 Live Crew) Wendy plainly states that she's "on hiatus," and has an aura of resignation about her when she's on camera.

The British band The Mekons, regarded for their politically astute songwriting, recorded a song in 1990 called "Club Mekon" and its refrain is, "this world belongs to them/well they can keep it." This sentiment seem to echo Wendy's feelings towards the music industry and perhaps pop culture in general at this time.

Wendy had ceased to perform at this point, leaving the Plasmatics and *W.O.W.* to her past. She really seemed to be pushed into a corner in terms of her music career by this juncture. Record companies weren't interested in her and venues didn't want to book her for fear of local law enforcement, and radio stations never were especially supportive of her even during the days when the Plasmatics played sold-out concerts. As Swenson told *Killdren*: "We had agreed with each other that if there came a time where compromise became a necessity that we'd hang it up. And that's what we did."

As for her disinterest in performing again, Roger Caitlin, writing in an April 27, 1998 *Hartford Courant* article reported that Wendy succinctly remarked to a Storrs acquaintance who asked if she missed the rock star lifestyle: "No, I have memories. I have good memories" and didn't say much more about the subject.

A Place Where There Is No Self, Only Calm

In the Connecticut woods near the home she had shared with Rod Swenson, Wendy committed suicide by shooting herself on April 6, 1998.

She had attempted to take her life twice before; once by plunging a knife into her chest. The knife became lodged in her sternum and, changing her mind, she called Swenson who took her to a hospital. Another time Wendy attempted suicide by overdosing on ephedrine. According to Joy Williams, writing in SPIN, when this happened, Swenson called Poison Control from a pay phone because Wendy didn't want the call to be traced back to their house. If the authorities found out that she tried to commit suicide, Wendy thought they would hospitalize her and she was very afraid of being institutionalized.

Swenson had spent a substantial amount of time in the years leading up to the last day of Wendy's life trying to convince her to keep on living. At one point, according to Joy Williams, writing in SPIN, Swenson told Wendy she shouldn't kill herself during the winter because that was before the woodland animals came out and found enough to eat. Wendy agreed with this and was persuaded to keep on living for the time being. After her third and final attempt, when Swenson found Wendy's body, there were nut shells close by her on a rock, giving the impression that the last thing Wendy did was feed squirrels.

On the last day of her life, Wendy shut off her phone line and ended the mail delivery that she had at Steve Gabriel's Guide Lines Tattoo and took her fax machine, a screenplay she wrote called "Revenge of the Gland Snatchers," a teapot she had since the

Plasmatics days, some clothes and a .38 handgun she found next to Gabriel's bed.

Richie Stotts recalls how he heard about Wendy's death: "I came home from work one night at 10:00 and a reporter tracked me down and told me about it. It was totally shocking. If she got killed by a car or had some medical thing that would have been shocking. That she killed herself didn't make sense to me. It still doesn't make any sense to me. It's too jarring. The dots don't connect for the Wendy I knew. She had taken care of herself, didn't drink, eating wheatgrass and she wanted to look good, she was in the entertainment field, she had done some TV. It didn't make a lot of sense to me.

"The last time I saw her physically..." Stotts thinks back in my conversation with him in the summer of 2019 "...when the core Plasmatics ended around 1984, I didn't speak to her until four or five years later. I had a band called The Richie Stotts Experience or Richie Stotts, I'm trying to remember what I called it. We were a three-piece band, Chris Romanelli was playing with us and we were opening for The Ramones at Irving Plaza and Joey Ramone said to me "Hey Richie, let's get Wendy to come out and sing; let's get Wendy," and I was like... I don't know because maybe things weren't so great between Rod Swenson and me; we hadn't spoken. So Joey called up Rod and invited him and Wendy down and they said ok. So we were doing a New Year's Eve show and Wendy joined us and sang "Masterplan." It was like old times, there was no ill feelings or anything like that."

In Jason Webber's interview with Rod Swenson from *Noisey/VICE*, Webber asks if Swenson was angry with Wendy for ending her own life: "Anger, in any case for someone who takes this ultimate step, is not something I would readily understand," Swenson said. "Utterly deep and inexpressible grief and loss. But anger, no. I will tell you that while she was here she lived with an authenticity that few can rival, and this, I think was a goal in life she set with a determination at a young age. Despite remarkable hurdles, I believe she achieved this goal. Her work and her legacy speak for itself."

When Jean Beauvoir heard about Wendy committing suicide he was "... really saddened, but in a strange way I kind of understood," he says. "Wendy lived for what she did and the fans were her life, the whole motivation – she'd get up and eat and do what she did but the whole motivation was the Plasmatics. Once the lineup broke up, things went in a strange direction for her. She didn't quite get the same appreciation, she got kind of forced into a solo thing. After that she wasn't playing anymore and some people can't stand that – to lose that in a way they never had before. I wasn't there at the end but I'm sure she'd be really welcome now."

Perhaps ironically, Tammy Wynette also died (from Thrombus) on April 6, 1998.

When she died, Wendy was a little over a month shy of her 49th birthday. Sources have said she hated the idea of getting old. Given that she was so devoted to fitness and healthy eating – two things about her body and life that she could control – aging and the possibility of contracting an age-related disease may have been too overwhelming for her.

Maybe Wendy had difficulty adjusting to a "normal" life in the quiet daily pace of a small town like Storrs. She had been internationally famous, performing in front of adoring crowds. In Storrs, she got fired for showing up late to work in a health food store.

Wendy may have just given up on a world that wouldn't listen to her. She tried to alert the world to global warming with *Maggots* but despite some good reviews it didn't really find an audience. As previously stated, venues were afraid of local police action if they booked her. Could she have switched gears and done, say, spoken word performances or written a memoir? It's hard to say. Wendy had stated in 1980 that she "didn't like art" and maybe her not having a typical artist's ego and sense of self made her give up on life. Given Wendy's devotion to uncompromising, heavy rock 'n' roll and her disdain for art, one can imagine her not being particularly interested in other forms of expression.

The note Wendy left was poignantly contemplative and describes her philosophy towards suicide in general. As she stated in this excerpt:

"I don't believe that people should take their own lives without deep and thoughtful reflection over a considerable period of time. I do believe strongly, however, that the right to do so is one of the

most fundamental rights that anyone in a free society should have. For me, much of the world makes no sense, but my feelings about what I am doing ring loud and clear to an inner ear and a place where there is no self, only calm."

Wendy asked for no memorial services and was cremated on April 13, 1998.

How did Wendy go from being so very much alive and health conscious to not wanting to live any longer? Was mental health counseling ever even a possibility for her? Maybe not. Wendy hated drugs; it's possible she wouldn't have taken prescribed anti-depressants. This stalwart anti-drug stance possibly prevented her from taking medication that might have helped her cope with everyday life. Did her abandoning music and performing contribute to her depression? Maybe.

Rod Swenson issued a press release on April 7 1998, following Wendy's suicide, in which he stated: "She felt, in effect, she'd peaked and didn't care to live in a world in which she was uncomfortable and below peak any longer," Swenson continued to say, "She found the ordinary 'hypocrisies of life' as she called them, excruciatingly hard to deal with."

About a month after Wendy's suicide, The *Hartford Courant* reported on a memorial service for Wendy that was held at CBGB. Rod Swenson addressed the crowd and said: "There was no other place where we felt we could do this," perhaps referring to how Wendy first established herself with the Plasmatics onstage at the legendary punk venue.

Having run away from home at age 16, Wendy had a palpable distance from her family. She reportedly had some contact with her mother after she became famous and a female relative had a daughter named Wendy, but none of her family members came to the CBGB memorial.

Richie Stotts, Wes Beech, Chosei Funahara, Stu Deutsch, Jean Beauvoir and T.C. Tolliver performed Plasmatics songs at Wendy's memorial, taking turns at vocals. Beauvoir sang lead on "Masterplan." After the six-song set, Joey Ramone greeted Stotts and said, "Richie, you gave it your all!"

On April 24, 2016, Wendy was inducted into the Rochester Music Hall of Fame. Rod Swenson accepted the award. At the ceremony, a band was assembled to play Plasmatics songs. It consisted of Wes Beech on guitar, T.C. Tolliver on drums and local musicians John Lalopa and Darren Pilato on second guitar and bass. the Plasmatics went through many personnel changes in their history but Beech was the longest running member as he played guitar not only on every Plasmatics album but also in Wendy's solo bands. Liz O' Brien, from Rochester-based band The Cheetah Whores sang "Living Dead" and "Brain Dead." Cherie Currie, lead singer of the early '70s all-girl rock group The Runaways, sang "Butcher Baby" and "The Damned." (In an odd connection to Wendy, Currie had become known for making ice sculptures with a chainsaw).

In an article in the April 27 1998 issue of *The Hartford Courant*, written by Roger Caitlin, Rod Swenson reflected on how history would regard Wendy "Sometimes with people's death comes the recognition [finally]. That's the only thing that gets me emotional," he said. "That's the way it always is. That's the odd thing about death. Part of it seems to be, when people who are radical die, then people who were marginalizing them tend to be more sympathetic because they're safe now. You can package them, put them in a place.

"True radicals - and Wendy was a true radical," Swenson continues, "she was a person that would do anything to see what it was like - those people are scary people to some. And rightfully so, because they're right on the edge."

Oedipus, the program director at radio station WBCN in Boston, said "Wendy taught us not to take ourselves too seriously. She expanded our concepts of life and art, and that is a life worth celebrating."

In 2017 a band was formed in San Francisco called the Slapmatics – a Plasmatics tribute band put together by Beth Allen, who would "channel" Richie Stotts while playing guitar in the band. The Slapmatics' 'Wendy' was vocalist Chelsea Rose. The band only existed for about a year, playing a small amount of shows, but the members of the band felt strongly about paying tribute to Wendy and the Plasmatics.

"What I wanted to bring to the table, what I admired most about Wendy O. was her authenticity," Rose said in a 2020 interview. "She was such a *real* person and I could really relate how she left her small town because she felt out of place. She brought such a real raw power to what she did, whether it was her singing and the music or her theatrics I just feel like that's what I wanted to get across to people on stage. Beth Allen asked me if I would front the Slapmatics and I said, 'give me 24 hours to think about it' because it struck me as a tall order to fill. I thought about it and I thought, "You know, she really stands for freedom and that's exactly how I feel about life too, so I thought, why not be brave and take a chance?"

"I think the first immediate thing you notice about Wendy is her raw sexuality and the power that she, had--being able to express herself the way she wanted to," says Rose "And then when you get past the image and then you get down to the actual songs you know that she's singing about corruption and standing against the status quo. I really related to that."

"To me Wendy's just such a goddess," said Beth Allen, also in a 2020 interview. "She just appeals to me. She was trying to change the world for better. She just had her politics and she didn't give a shit. This is what she believes in."

"I did college radio for years and people don't know the Plasmatics like they know, say the Ramones or the Misfits, "Allen says. "The Slapmatics were only around for a year. We were just doing it for fun. There was no way in hell we could ever *be* the Plasmatics, but my intention has always been; if I could turn one teenage kid or someone in their twenties on to the awesomeness of the Plasmatics and Wendy O. Williams then it's worth it."

With a tone of reverence, Allen says: "I love telling the story of what happened in Milwaukee. How most people would have just paid the fine and scooted, but Wendy said, "fuck you – I'm going to sue the police department!"

"I never saw the Plasmatics but I did see Wendy in L.A. in 1987 on the *Maggots* tour," Allen recalls. "My friend Scooter did see the Plasmatics and when Wendy chain sawed the guitar in half he caught the guitar and had it on his wall. So when we went to see Wendy O.

he fucking caught the guitar *again*. I was like "Give it to me – you already have one! And he said no! So he has two."

"People often say; "What would Jesus do?"Reflects Allen. "I often think, 'What would Wendy O. do?' Because Wendy O. stood up for her beliefs and principles and she was ethical. I've always thought of her as kind of the Mother Theresa of punk rock. She's just fucking cool. I was really sad when she killed herself but I was kind of like, 'I get it – the world's just shit.' I got a tattoo of a chainsaw for her that says "In loving memory of Wendy. O."

Acknowledgements

Many thanks to Emily Morry of the Local History & Genealogy Division, Central Library of Rochester and Monroe County.

Thank you to Neal Smith www.nealsmithrocks.com, Richard Cummins, Susan Mainzer, Simon Reynolds, Mark Kahn and Aeric Schaubroek and Ira Robbins for research assistance.

Discography

Plasmatics
Meet the Plasmatics, released by Vice Squad 1979 VS-106ESP
Track List
Sometimes I
Won't You?
Want You Baby
Credits
Wendy Orlean Williams –Vocals
Chosei Funahara – Bass
Butch Star—Cover photo and design
Wes Beech—Rhythm guitar
Richie Stotts—Lead guitar, rhythm guitar , songwriting
Stu Deutsch—Drums
Stellar Axeman—Producer
Rod Swenson—Management, concept,songwriting
Ed Stasium—Engineer
John Shiek—Assistant engineer
Greg Calbi--Mastering

New Hope For The Wretched LP released by Stiff America USE9
1980
Track List
Tight Black Pants
Monkey Suit
Living Dead
Test Tube Babies
Won't You
Concrete Shoes
Squirm (Live)
Want You Baby
Dreamlover
Sometimes I
Corruption
Butcher Baby

Credits
Wendy O. Williams –vocals
Rod Swenson—concept, management, mixing
Wes Beech –rhythm guitar
Richie Stotts – lead guitar
Jean Beauvoir—bass
Stu Deutsch—drums, electronic drums
Jimmy Miller—producer
Ed Stasium—mixing
Trevor Hallesy—engineer
Butch Star—photography

Monkey Suit 7" 45 RPM single Stiff Records Buy 91 1980
Track List
Monkey Suit/Squirm (Live)
Credits
Wendy O. Williams –vocals/writing
Wes Beech—Rhythm guitar
Richie Stotts—Lead guitar
Jean Beauvoir—Bass Guitar
Stu Deutsch--Drums
Stellar Axeman—writing
Butch Star—phtotography

Plasmatics Butcher Baby 7" Stiff Records Buy 76 1980
Track List
Butcher Baby/Tight Black Pants
Credits
Wendy O. Williams – vocals, chainsaw
Richie Stotts—Lead Guitar
Wes Beech—Rhythm Guitar
Jean Beauvoir—Bass
Stu Deutsch—Drums
Rod Swenson—Art Direction, Plasmatics concept , management
Butch Star—Photography (front cover)
Allen Tannenbaum—Photography (back cover)
Jimmy Miller—Producer "Butcher Baby"

Trevor Hallesy—Engineer "Butcher Baby"
Ed Stasium—Mixing "Butcher Baby," Engineer "Tight Black Pants"
Rod Swenson , Ed Stasium—Producers "Tight Black Pants"

Beyond The Valley of 1984 LP released on Stiff America WOW II 1981
Track List
Incantation
Masterplan
Headbanger
Summer Nite
Nothing
Fast Food Service
Hit Man (Live Milan)
Living Dead
Sex Junkie
Plasma Jam (Live Milan)
Pig is A Pig
Credits
Wendy O. Williams—Vocals
Rod Swenson—Concept, management, producer
Richie Stotts—Lead guitar
Wes Beech-Rhythm guitar
Jean Beauvoir—Bass, piano, synthesizer
Neal Smith—Drums
Butch Star—Photography
Eddie Ciletti--Engineer

Metal Priestess EP Stiff America WOW666 1981
Track List
Lunacy
Doom Song
Sex Junkie
Black Leather Monster
12 Noon
Masterplan
Credits

Rod Swenson—Concept, Management, Producer
Dan Hartman—Producer, Engineer
Richie Stotts—Lead guitar, songwriting
Wes Beech—Rhythm guitar, keyboards, songwriting
Chris Romanelli—Bass
Leslie Cabarga- Cover art

Stand by Your Man 7" Bronze BRO 151 1982
Track Listing
Stand By Your Man
No Class
Masterplan
Credits
Wendy O. Williams – Vocals
Lemmy Kilmister – Bass, producer, vocals
Rod Swenson –Producer
Dan Hartman – Producer
The Company (8) –Producer
Richie Stotts – Lead Guitar
Wes Beech – Rhythm guitar
Phil Taylor – Drums
Butch Star -- Photography
Coup D' Etat Capitol ST-12237 1982
Track Listing
Put Your Love in Me
Stop
Rock 'n' Roll
Lightning Breaks
No Class
Mistress of Taboo
Country Fairs
Path of Glory
Just Like on TV
The Damned
Credits
Wendy O. Williams—Vocals
Richie Stotts—Lead guitar

Wes Beech—Rhythm guitar
Chris Romanelli – Bass, keyboards
T.C. Tolliver – Drums
Dieter Dirks – Producer
Rod Swenson—Concept, management

Wendy O. Williams /W.O.W
W.O.W   Passport Records PB6034 released 1984
Track Listing
I Love Sex (And Rock And Roll)
It's My Life
Priestess
Thief In The Night
Opus In Cm7
Ready To Rock
Bump And Grind
Legends Never Die
Ain't None Of Your Business
Credits
Acoustic Guitar—Micki Free (track B3)
Bass Guitar – Reginald Van Helsing
Concept by – Rod Swenson
Design, Cover Photography by – Butch Star
Drums – Eric Carr (track B3), T.C. Tolliver (tracks A1 to B2, B4)
Engineer – Frank Fillipetti
Engineer (2nd) – Tom Roberts
Engineer (Assistant) – Billy Miranda, Moira Marquis, Tom Brick
Guitar – Paul Stanley (track B1)
Lead Guitar – Ace Frehley (track B2), Michael Ray (tracks A1, A3,B1, B3, B4), Wes Beech (track A2)
Lead Vocals – Wendy O. Williams
Management – Rod Swenson
Mastered by – George Marino
Piano—Mitch Weissman (track A5)
Producer – Gene Simmons
Rhythm Guitar – Wes Beech

Kommander of Kaos   Gigasaurus Records GIGAC 8948 released 1986
Track Listing
Hoy Hey (Live To Rock)
Pedal To The Metal
Goin' Wild
Ain't None of Your Business (Live)
Party
Jailbait
Bad Girl
Fight For The Right
(Work That Muscle) F**k That Booty
Credits
Wendy O. Williams – vocals
Wes Beech – Associate Producer, Guitar
Eric Carr – Composer
"Fast" Eddie Clarke – Composer
Peter Cronin – Back Cover
Lemmy Kilmister –Composer
Andy Krehm _- CD Master Tape
George Marino – Mastering
John Michaels – Cover Photo
Michael Ray—Guitar, Rhythm Guitar, Background Vocals
Mark Shane – Assistant Engineer
Greg Smith – Bass, Background Vocals
Rod Swenson – Audio Production, Concept
Phil "Philthy Animal" Taylor – Composer
Al "Turn It Up" Theurer -- Audio Engineer
T.C.Tolliver – Drums, Background vocals.

Wendy O.Williams/ Plasmatics Maggots: The Record WOW Records PAL 1230 Profile Records PAL 1230 released 1987
Tracks
Overture
Introduction (Narrator)
You're A Zombie
The White's Apartment (Narrative)

Full Meal Diner (Narrative)
The White's Apartment (Narrative)
The Day of the Humans is Gone
The Central Research Laboratory
Valerie and Bruce on the Phone
Destroyer
The White's Apartment (Narrative)
Bruce's Bedroom (Narrative)
Brain Dead
The White's Apartment (Narrative)
Bruce's Bedroom (Narrative)
Propagators
The White's Bedroom (Narrative)
Fire Escape (Narrative)
Finale

Credits

Wendy O. Williams -- Vocals
Chris "Junior" Romanelli – Bass Guitar
Chris Romanelli, Michael Ray, Ray Callahan, Stellar Axeman, Wes Beech—Chorus
Rod Swenson – Concept, Management
Butch Star – Cover Design
Ray Callahan –Drums
John Smith – Engineer
Al Theurer – Second Assistant
Lawrence "The Peet Factor" Peet – Assistant Engineer
Wes Beech – Lead Guitar
Eric Karalis –Cover Painting
John Michaels – Photography
Rod Swenson – Producer
Wes Beech – Associate Producer
Marketing and Promotion—Second Vision Ltd.
Wes Beech – Rhythm Guitar
Michael Ray – Rhythm and Lead Guitar
Andy Bleiberg, James Geerth, Jeanine P. Morick, Jeff Grigak, Scott Harlan, Stellar Axeman, Suzanne Bedford, Tony Marzocco–voice actors, Ray, Swenson, Beech -- Writing

Deffest and Baddest Profile Records (serial number unavailable) released 1988
Track Listing
Rulers of Rock
$10,000,00 Winner
Super Jock Guy
Early Days
The Humpty Song
Know Wa'am Saying
On the IRT
Lies
La La Land
Laffin' and Scratching
Credits
Wendy O. Williams – Vocals
Katrina Astrin – Guitar, Background Vocals
Wes Beech – Associate Producer, Guitar, Rhythm Guitar
Andy Khrem – Mastering
John Michaels – Cover Photo
Phil Phisterer – Engineer, Mixing Engineer
Butch Star – Artwork, Cover Design
LaDonna Sullivan – Background Vocals
Rod Swenson – Producer
Craig White – Engineer

Compliations
Wendy O. Williams Fuck You!!! And Loving It Powerage (serial number unavailable) released 1988 (re-released 2003)
Tack Listing
Tight Black Pants Live (with a special rehearsal segment from 1977) (from *New Hope for the Wretched*)
Butcher Baby (from *New Hope for the Wretched*)
Sex Junkie Live (from *Beyond the Valley of 1984*)
A Pig is a Pig (from *Beyond the Valley of 1984*)
It's My Life"(from *WOW* and the Reform School Girls soundtrack)
Hoy Hey (Live to Rock) (from *Kommander of Kaos*)
Goin' Wild (from *Kommander of Kaos*)

You're a Zombie (from *Maggots: The Record*)
Propagators (from *Maggots: The Record*)
Know W'am Sayn (from *Deffest! and Baddest!*)

Plasmatics Coup de Grace Plasmatics Media/ High Roller records (serial number unavailable) Released 2002
Track Listing
Put Your Love in Me (Stotts, Swenson) - 4:13
Stop (Beech, Swenson) - 4:34
Rock 'n' Roll (Stotts, Swenson) - 3:58
Just Like on TV (Beech, Swenson) - 4:04
Uniformed Guards (Stotts, Swenson) - 4:27
No Class (Clarke, Kilmister, Taylor) - 2:09
Mistress of Passion (Stotts, Swenson) - 3:43
Lightning Breaks (Beech, Swenson) - 3:42
Path of Glory (Stotts, Swenson) - 5:00
Country Fairs (Stotts, Swenson) - 4:08
The Damned (Romanelli, Swenson) - 3:54
Credits
Wendy O. Williams – Vocals
Rod Swenson – Producer
Dan Hartman – Producer
Chris Romanelli – Bass
Riche Stotts – Lead Guitar
Wes Beech – Lead Guitar
Joey Reese – Drums
Andy Krehm -- Mastering

Wendy O. Williams Fuck 'n'Roll (Live Album) MVD Audio – MVD6980LP released April 2016
Recorded Live November 24 1984 at at L'Amour, Brooklyn NY
Track Listing
Fuck and Roll
Ain't None of Your Business
Bump and Grind
Credits

Wendy O. Wiliams -- Vocals
Greg "Bootyman" Smith – Bass
Rod Swenson – Concept, Management
 T.C. "Big Gun" Tolliver -- Drums [Skins]
Randy Ezratty – Engineer
Mark Shane Engineer [Assistant]
Al Theurer – Engineer [Mix]
Michael "Deadly Axe" Ray – Lead Guitar
Isaac Betesh – Mastered By
CJIII – Mastered By [Vinyl]
Butch Star, Rod Swenson – Photography
Big "Bull" Dozer – Producer
Wes "Son of a" Beech – Rhythm Guitar

Put Your Love In Me – Love Songs For The Apocalypse CD released 2002, Plasmatics Media (serial number unavailable) Track Listing
"Fuck That Booty" – (From the *Kommander of Kaos* album)
"Put Your Love in Me" – (From the *Coup de Grace* album)
"Fast Food Service" - (From the *New Hope for the Wretched* album)
 "Bump and Grind" - (From the *WOW* album)
 "Sex Junkie" - (From the *Beyond the Valley of 1984* album)
 "Black Leather Monster" - (From the *Metal Priestess* EP)
 "Jailbait" - (From the *Kommander of Kaos* album)
 "Party" - (From the *Kommander of Kaos* album)
"I Love Sex (And Rock and Roll)" - (From the *WOW* album)
"Dream Lover" - From the *New Hope for the Wretched* album)
"The Humpty Song" - (From the *Deffest! and Baddest!* album)

Final Days--Anthems For The Apocalypse released by Gigasaurus Records 2002 (serial number unavailable) Track Listing
"The Doom Song" - (From the *Metal Priestess* EP)
"Stop" - (From the *Coup de Grace* album)
"Brain Dead" - (From the *Maggots: The Record* album)
"Masterplan" - (From the *Beyond the Valley of 1984* album)
"Just Like on TV" - (From the *Coup de Grace* album)

"Propagators" - (From the *Maggots: The Record* album)
"Uniformed Guards" - (From the *Coup de Grace* album)
"Opus in Cm7" - (From the *WOW* album)
"Lies" - (From the *Deffest! and Baddest!* album)
"The Damned" - (From the *Coup de Grace* album)
"A Pig is a Pig" - (From the *Beyond the Valley of 1984* album)
"Finale" - (From the *Maggots: The Record* album)
Credits
Wendy O. Williams –Vocals
Jean Beauvoir – Bass
Wes Beech – Associate Producer, Composer, Rhythm Guitar, Keyboard, Background Vocals
Tom Brick – Assistant Enginer
Ray Callahan – Drums, Background Vocals
Eddie Ciletti – Mixing
Frank Filipetti –Engineer
Dan Hartman – Engineer, Producer
Ted Jensen – Mastering
Andy Krehm – Mastering
George Marino – Mastering
Moira Marquis – Assistant Engineer
Billy Miranda – Assistant Engineer
Phil Phisterer – Engineer

Michael Ray – Guitar, Background Vocals
Joey Reese—Drums
Tom Roberts – Engineer
Chris Romanelli— Bass, Keyboards, Background Vocals
Jo Smith – Engineer
Neal Smith – Drums
Richie Stotts – Guitar, Composer
Rod Swenson – Composer, Concept, Producer
Al Theurer – Engineer
T.C. Tolliver – Drums
Reginald Van Helsing – Bass
Mitch Weissman – Keyboards, Piano
Craig White – Engineer

About the Author

Robin Eisgrau has been writing about music and cultural subjects for many years. She has held editorial positions at Paper, Seventeen, Time Out New York, NET, and CMJ New Music Report.

Her byline has appeared in The New York Post, The Village Voice, Sky Magazine UK, The Boston Phoenix, Interview, JC Downtown, Alternative Press and the arts website offoffoff.com. She writes two blogs: Plate Envy, about food and related subjects, and Focus and Temper where she discusses music and personal reflections. With Richard John Cummins she co-authored Name, Rank Rock and Roll: Famous Musicians Who Served In The Military, also published by New Haven Publishing.

Eve of Destruction